YEOVIL

IN THE GREAT WAR
1914-1918

Front Cover: Photographed in March 1918, just before they left for the Western Front, are Reg Sweet (standing) and Bert Jennings, two 18 years-old Yeovilians, both of whom were conscripted into the Army in October 1917, trained together on Salisbury Plain, and served together in 'A' Company, 2nd Battalion of the Wiltshire Regiment, but sadly only one returned home to Yeovil. Reg was awarded the Military Medal for carrying messages under heavy fire, was badly wounded in the Battle of the River Selle east of Cambrai, on 20 October 1918, and returned home to Yeovil in January 1919. Sadly Bert was killed in action on 31 May 1918 and lies at rest in Chambrecy British Cemetery, near Reims.

YEOVIL

IN THE GREAT WAR
1914-1918

JACK SWEET

FONTHILL

ACKNOWLEDGEMENTS

Many thanks to my cousin Annette White for the loan of the photograph of her grandfather Caleb Edney Newis, who died on the Somme in September 1916.

My great appreciation and thanks to Emma Slee, the editor of the *Western Gazette* for permission to use articles from the *Western Gazette* and *Yeovil Times* in this book. A special thank you to my wife, Margaret, for her patience and tolerance during the many years of my writing adventures.

Fonthill Media Limited
www.fonthillmedia.com
office@fonthillmedia.com

First published 2014

Typeset in 10pt on 13pt Sabon LT
Printed and bound in England

Connect with us
 facebook.com/fonthillmedia 🐦 twitter.com/fonthillmedia

CONTENTS

INTRODUCTION

IT'S WAR!

The history of the First World War, or Great War as it was originally known, which broke out in August 1914 and lasted four terrible years, has been, and will no doubt, continue to be the source of thousands of books and articles and millions of words. Sufficient to say that the first decade of the twentieth century witnessed the rapid build up of tensions and rivalries between the major European powers, and all that was needed was a spark to ignite the flames of war. This came on 28 June 1914 in Sarajevo with the assignation by a Serb nationalist of the heir the Austro-Hungarian throne, the Archduke Franz Ferdinand and his wife Sophie.

Demands were made, alliances were called and war was declared between the German – Austro-Hungarian axis and its allies, and the alliance of Russia and France. When Germany invaded neutral Belgium on 3 August 1914 to strike at France, Great Britain, which had guaranteed Belgium's neutrality since 1839, declared war on Germany the following day. No one in Yeovil, or indeed across the nation, on that summer day could in their wildest nightmares have imagined the four long terrible years which would follow - because it was bound to be over by Christmas!

Yeovil in the Great War 1914 –1918 is not a history of the conflict and it is not even an attempt to write one, but is a personal look back to the life of the town of my birth and its people through those momentous years, and includes some of the articles I contributed to the former *Yeovil Times* and the *Western Gazette,*

Bristolian, Lance Corporal Bert Harper, 'A' Company, 2nd Battalion, Wiltshire Regiment, who when my father Reg Sweet was badly wounded on 20 October 1918, carried him under fire and in great personal danger to a forward casualty dressing station and thereby saved his life. Thankfully, Bert survived the war.

1914

THE LAST DAYS OF PEACE

On the afternoon of Tuesday 4 August 1914, the Prime Minister, Mr Herbert Asquith, announced to a packed House of Commons that the assurances sought from Germany to respect Belgium's neutrality, following the German declaration of war on France, had not been received, Belgium had been invaded and as a consequence Great Britain had declared war on Germany. For Yeovilians and for untold millions the war of unimagined ferocity would change forever the world they had known. So let's take a quick look back at Yeovil during those high summer days of late July and early August 1914 before, in the memorable words of Sir Edward Grey; 'The lamps are going out all over Europe; we shall not see them lit again in our lifetime.'

On Wednesday 29 July, the body of Lady Harbin, one of the founders of St Michael and All Angels' Church, was brought from Haselmere in Surrey, accompanied by mourners in motor cars, and laid to rest at the east end of the Lady Chapel in ground set aside for the burial of the founders and patrons of the church. The afternoon funeral was the first to take place in the church and was attended by a large number of mourners and parishioners.

The following day the choirboys of St John's Church enjoyed their annual outing to Weymouth, partly paid for by an organ recital by their choir master and organist, Mr Risdon, and where they were provided 'with dinner and tea and spent a very happy day'. Two days later, twenty members of the St John's Men's Bible Class travelled by motor charabanc for a day's outing to Wedmore and on the way paid a visit to Wells Cathedral.

On Saturday 1 August, St Andrew's Church choir went to Weymouth, enjoyed a trip around Portland Harbour, visited a battleship, had tea at Lumley's Restaurant, and arrived home at 9.30 p.m. after 'an enjoyable day'. The Yeovil and District (North Road) Homing Society raced their pigeons from Gloucester to Yeovil but the poor weather conditions made it a very hard flight back to the home lofts in Yeovil. During that evening Mr E. Shettle was motoring towards the town along the Preston Road and had just passed Grove Avenue when the front off side tyre burst with a terrific report. The car became unmanageable and skidded around till the bonnet faced the direction from which the car had come, the tail end being thrown against Mr Hunt's wall with considerable force, smashing the tail lamp and damaging the off side back wheel. Luckily Mr Shettle escaped unhurt.

That first Saturday in August saw a full cricket calendar. Yeovil Thursday won at Evershot, 59 runs to 34, with Thursday's G. Priddle taking 6 wickets for 9. This made up for the thrashing the Thursdays received two days before at the hands of Compton Park who won by 124 runs to 59; even so G. Priddle took 5 wickets for 28. On the 'Whistles' ground, Yeovil Weslyans beat St Ivel A by the narrow margin of 3 runs, the low scores of 30 and 27 being blamed on the poor condition of the wicket. At home St Ivel (Yeovil) played Marston Magna but the 'Ivelites' were dismissed all out for 27 against Marston's 39; once again the low scores were attributed to the condition of the pitch. At Taunton, Somerset beat Derbyshire by 6 wickets.

On Sunday 2 August Mrs Seymour, the leader of the Congregational Church Primary Department, retired after fifty years of working for the Sunday School. She was presented with a large photograph of the infant class and a 'purse of gold' from the teachers and helpers of the Sunday School.

During the last week of peace, a party of West Indians led by Staff Captain Narraway visited the Yeovil Salvation Army Temple and the services of celebration included a special open-air meeting in the Triangle.

The Yeovil Borough Council's last peacetime meeting was held on 13 July and the reports in the local newspapers give no hint of the coming crisis. Business included a discussion on the town water supply and a suggested new reservoir off the West Coker Road, arrangements to inspect the Eastland Housing Estate, an insanitary building in Middle Street, West Hendford drainage, repairs to the Sherborne Road drinking fountain, the preparation of a town planning scheme, the purchase of apparatus to examine diphtheria swabs etc., the Medical Officer of Health's monthly report and so on. Among those present at the meeting were the Town Clerk, Mr H. C. C. Batten and Councillor E. J. Farr, but by the time the Council met again both had left to join their regiments, both would be wounded, and both would return to public life in the town.

At the last peacetime town magistrates' court, an impecunious local hairdresser, was fined 2s 6d for using indecent language, but told the Bench that if he paid the fine there and then, 'he would not be able to go to the fête', and asked if he could pay the following Saturday - the request was granted.

The 'fête' the defendant was so anxious to attend, was the Conservative and Unionist 'Fête of the West,' one of the highlights of the year, to be held on Tuesday 4 August at Yew Tree Close Park. There would be a Flower Show, Athletic Sports, Daylight Carnival with 'pretty scenes and tableaux,' a Grand Procession from Wyndham Fields led by bands and lodges of the Blue Marines, Variety Entertainments by 'Clever Star Artists,' a Grand Display by Brock of Crystal Palace fame, illumination of the Grounds and performances by the Yeovil Military and Crewkerne Town Bands. Yeovil's MP, the Hon. Aubrey Herbert and George Lloyd Esq. MP, would speak at the Fête. Cheap railway tickets were available for patrons from all stations within forty miles of Yeovil.

First Prize cart at the Conservative and Unionist Fête on Tuesday 4 August 1914.

Despite the rapidly unfolding crisis, the fête went ahead, but the party political element was removed and instead, patriotic letters were read from the two MPs, now present in the House of Commons. The *Western Gazette* reported that numbers were down on the previous year and this probably reflected the 'acute tension in the country before the declaration of war and partly no doubt to the heavy rain which fell early in the afternoon'.

Under the headline 'The Menace of War,' the *Western Gazette* reported that on Sunday 2 August 'the services at all places of worship in the town were of an intercessionary character, prayers being offered for the continuance of peace'.

Monday, 3 August was the Bank Holiday and no doubt with the closure of shops, offices and factories, many townsfolk were looking forward to a trip to the seaside or a visit to out-of-town friends or relations. However, many were to be disappointed when, with the exception of those to Weymouth and West Bay, all railway excursions from Yeovil Town and Pen Mill Stations were cancelled in response to the growing fears of the coming conflict.

Within weeks of the declaration of war, local army and naval reservists had been recalled to their regiments or ships, Special Reservists, Territorials and the first volunteers for Kitchener's Army had left. Still they wouldn't be away for long because hadn't everyone said that the war would be over by Christmas!

AUGUST

It goes without saying, that the declaration of war on Germany on 4 August 1914 sent Yeovil as well as the rest of the country, into patriotic mood.

E (Yeovil) Company of the 1st (West) Somerset Battalion of the National Reserve, had already paraded in the Borough on the morning of 3 August, and travelled to Taunton to join the rest of the Battalion where they were presented with their Colours. The Yeovil Company, or 'straw hat brigade', a nickname they bore with some pride on account of most of them wearing straw hats, returned home that evening to await further orders for the mobilization.

The Somerset Light Infantry's Territorial 5th Battalion were halfway through their fortnight's annual camp at Bulford, and moved down to Devonport within days of the declaration of war. Members of the Yeovil TA Company who had returned home after a week's training, were immediately recalled and left Yeovil Town Station for Devonport to the ringing cheers of a crowd of well-wishers on Thursday morning 6 August. The Battalion would soon be sent to India to replace the Regular 2nd Battalion which returned for service on the Western Front.

When members of E (Yeovil) Company of the Somerset National Reserve paraded in the Borough on 3 August 1914, the day before war was declared, none could have foreseen the horrors to come.

Yeomanry cavalry troopers muster in the Borough.

D Squadron of the West Somerset Yeomanry cavalry were mustered and their preparations for active service were watched with much interest in Preston Grove outside the new armoury and HQ. The Squadron attended the Sunday morning service in St John's Church on 9 August and were cheered by a large crowd as they marched through Princes and High Streets to the Borough were they were dismissed. The following morning the Squadron paraded in High Street, and led by the Military Band, proceeded to the Town Station from whence they left to the loud cheers of townsfolk to join the Regiment at Winchester. The *Western Gazette* reported that as the Squadron assembled at the station, a train carrying German prisoners passed through.

During the days following the declaration of war, large numbers of horses were requisitioned by the military authorities from the surrounding farms and stables, assembled in Yeovil and sent by rail from Pen Mill and Town Stations to remount depots across the country.

Somerset Territorial, Jesse Chislett of Camborne Street, who had been charged with riding his bicycle without a light wrote that 'he could not attend before the magistrates as he was waiting mobilization'. However, this was treated as no excuse and he was fined one shilling in his absence. Sadly Jesse would be killed in France in April 1918 serving with the Worcester Regiment.

The Town Clerk, Mr Herbert C. C. Batten, who held the rank of captain in the 3rd Battalion of the Dorset Regiment, left for active service, and was soon followed by Councillor Ernest J. Farr, a National Reservist, both of whom would be wounded and both would return to office, Councillor Farr to be Mayor in 1921.

Yeovil's Member of Parliament, the Honorable Aubrey Herbert, despite very poor eye-sight which made him officially unfit for military service, bought a second lieutenant's uniform and joined the Irish Guards, as they boarded a troopship heading for France. He served with the Guards for several weeks before he was wounded, briefly taken prisoner, escaped, and returned to England. During the rest of the War he served with distinction in many official capacities mainly in the Near and Middle East. He remained as Yeovil's MP until his premature death in 1923.

Following the call for volunteers by the War Minister, Field Marshall Earl Kitchener, there was a large attendance at a meeting in the Town Hall called by the Mayor, Councillor Norman Buchanan, to raise recruits for the New Army Battalions, or 'Kitchener's Army' as it became known, and several recruitment mass meetings were held in the Borough. Within days, scores of recruits were enlisting in the new battalions.

On 27 August many of the 'straw hat brigade' of the National Reserve paraded in High Street outside the Town Hall, and following a rousing send-off they marched through cheering crowds to the Town Station. As they waited for the train to take them to the Somerset Light Infantry's Depot at Taunton, the Military band played suitable martial music and the contingent left to more cheers and the crash of fog detonators laid on the rails.

One story from the *Western Gazette* of 14 August, tells of a young fellow saying goodbye at the Town Station to some of his friends who had volunteered and as they were waiting for the train to Taunton, he was overheard by the Recruiting Sergeant accompanying his pals to say that he wished he was going with them. The sharp-eared and astute NCO asked the young fellow whether he meant what he said, and following his reply to the affirmative, the recruiting procedure swung into action. Borrowing a Bible from the station bookstall the Sergeant there and then swore in the young fellow before the Mayor who happened to be standing nearby. Within minutes of his attestation the new recruit had joined his friends and they all left for the Depot. Neither the young fellow nor his friends were named, and their fate remains unknown; I hope they all survived the war.

August had been a stupendous month, and at the time exhilarating, but despite the comings and goings of the military, recruiting, mass patriotic meetings and concerts, there was little sign of war in the columns of the local press. The shops appear to have opened as normal, and people went about their daily business.

A 'troublesome tramp' was given seven days in gaol for being drunk and disorderly in High Street, and a labourer was fined two shillings and sixpence for a similar offence. Another labourer was fined two shillings and six pence for not putting his dog's name on its collar, and it was suggested that the dog was used for poaching!

A horse drawing a trap bolted at the junction of High Street and Hendford and crashed into the shop window of the Rainbow Dye Works, smashing it to pieces. A three-year-old child who was riding in the trap was thrown into the shop amongst the shattered glass, but miraculously escaped injury; the horse was badly cut but the driver was unhurt.

A few days later on Sunday afternoon 21 August, a pony drawing a two-wheeled trap driven by Mr Trim of Yeovil Marsh, with Mr Rowsell from Mudford as passenger, went out of control as it turned into Princes Street from High Street and the trap was thrown against Mr Gaylard's shop window. Being Sunday, the shop was closed, and although the glass was completely broken the blind drawn down behind protected the display of glass and fancy goods. Despite the trap being badly damaged, neither the pony nor the occupants were injured.

Across the English Channel, battles raged between the huge armies of France and Germany, and the small but well-trained British Expeditionary Force (BEF) of regulars, territorials and reservists, fought to stem the German divisions pouring into neutral Belgium. The first battle between the British and German armies was fought on 23 August 1914 at the Belgian town of Mons and the first Yeovilian to die in war was twenty-eight-year-old Abendigo (Ben) Pike of the 1st Battalion of the Dorset Regiment, killed in action on the 24th, but his widow, who lived at 35 Great Western Terrace, with their three young children would not be told until the 24 September.

THE BELGIAN REFUGEES

The German invasion of neutral Belgium in August 1914 saw more than a million of its citizens fleeing the advancing armies, and the majority of the refugees crossed the borders into Holland, which remained neutral, and France. The British Government offered hospitality and over 20,000 Belgian refugees were welcomed to our shores. Following German guarantees of safety many returned to their homes in the occupied areas of Belgium, but the majority remained refugees for the rest of the war.

Following a request for assistance from the national Central Refugees Committee, a Yeovil Belgian Refugee Committee was set up under the chairmanship of the Mayor, Councillor Norman Buchanan, and Mr Charles Fox of Yew Tree Close made available 'Greystones' a large vacant house he owned on Hendford Hill, for the reception centre and temporary home supervised by a Roman Catholic Sister from Langport and a Sister from St Gilda's Convent in The Avenue.

The first party of refugee families comprising of fifty men, women and children, arrived at the Town Station during the afternoon of Saturday 3 October 1914, to be met by a large crowd of well wishers, and they were conveyed to 'Greystones' in horse carriages and their few possessions in bundles and wooden boxes were carried in a motor van. On arrival the refugees assembled in the large dining room where a hot meal awaited but there were some initial language problems as only three could speak and understand French, the rest being Flemish speakers, and there were no Flemish speakers amongst the reception committee or their supporters. However, this hurdle was overcome and within days several families were given accommodation in South Petherton and Stoke.

Another twenty-two refugees arrived at 'Greystones' on 23 October, and on 6 November the *Western Gazette* reported that 'A further party of refugees mostly women and children of the artisan class arrived at the Town Station on Friday afternoon when they were met by the Mayor and members of the Committee and driven to Greystones.'

A Sacred Concert in aid of funds for the Refugee Fund and arranged by Mr S. W. Bicknell, the local Salvation Army Bandmaster, was a sell-out in the Princes Street Assembly Rooms on Sunday evening 1 November.

By the beginning of 1915, there were 148 Belgian refugees living in Yeovil, and another 83 in the nearby villages. Their health was reported to be excellent and all but five of the men had found employment.

The War Relief Committee in London now asked Yeovil to help to accommodate several more families and a vacant furnished house owned by Mr E. H. Fletcher on Hendford Hill was immediately made available for the fifteen refugees who followed. During the coming months more families arrived and accommodation was found across the town.

Funds were being actively raised by the Yeovil Refugee Committee to cover of the necessary expenses on renting and furnishing houses, providing clothing and other necessities. Many of the Belgian ladies were now busy in making gloves, shirts, and much needed comforts for their countrymen serving in the trenches on the Western Front.

The first baby, a boy, was born on 4 May 1915 to Mons. and Madam Vormeerch. More refugees arrived in May and June 1915 and furnished houses were found at 12 Salisbury Terrace, Ford House, Reckleford and 70 Earle Street, and shortly after

'Greystones', Hendford Hill, the reception centre for the Belgian refugees and their temporary home.

their arrival a baby girl, Marie Elizabeth was born to Mons. and Madam Eyven at 12 Salisbury Terrace.

On 24 September 1915, the *Western Gazette* reported, 'Mons. Paquay and family, who have been resident at South Petherton, have removed to Yeovil and are now living at Rochester, Grove Avenue. Mons. Paquay is a professor of music and organist and it is hoped his services will be utilized.'

Sadly, on 25 October 1915, fifty-six-year-old Maria, the wife of Mons. Joseph Aspeslagh, died at 'Greystones' and was laid to rest at Yeovil Cemetery two days later.

By November 1915, some 250 Belgian refuges were living and being supported by the Yeovil Refugee Committee in and around the town and £2,577 had been raised to cover the necessary expenses.

Looking through the columns of the *Western Gazette*, apart from occasional reports of entertainments, fundraising and such like, the Belgian refugees slipped from the news, and it would appear they had become an accepted part of the local community.

On 30 October 1919, the Yeovil Refugee Committee held its final meeting. The Secretary reported that all the refugees had now left the town and district and returned home 'or were off the hands of the Committee'. The total income of the Relief Fund up to 20 June 1919 amounted to £8,587 16s 11d, (a very large sum at the time), of which all but £200 had been spent on items as varied as cash grants, rents, furnishing, heating, lighting, clothes and groceries. The Committee agreed that subject to consent of the Charity Commissioners the £200 be paid into the town's New Hospital Building Fund.

I believe the people of Yeovil and the surrounding villages can, even a century later, look back with pride at the welcome and hospitality given to several hundred men, women and children who had left everything they held dear following an unprovoked aggression.

THE FIRST WAR CHRISTMAS 1914

As 1914 drew to its close, the war which many optimists had predicted would be over by Christmas, was grinding remorselessly on as the opposing armies faced each other across the trenches on a battle front which stretched from the English Channel to the Swiss border; all the signs were that this was going to be a long war.

However, the *Western Gazette's* edition of 1 January 1915 looked back a week and recorded that:

Outwardly there was little to distinguish the Christmas of 1914 from others that have passed within memory, for again crowds of apparently light-hearted people thronged the streets of the town, shops were seemingly as full as ever of good cheer and customers, pedestrians made their way homewards with the same bulky parcels, the trains, crowded as ever, arrived with even more than seasonable punctuality, and the postman bore his usual burden on even more belated deliveries. Still with all these evidences of peace and goodwill, the shadow of war was forced upon the mind at every turn. Khaki at every turn, worn by men wearing the distinguishing badges of every branch of His Majesty's Army, and in several instances of men bearing traces of shot, shell and weather in the trenches. Passers-by recognizing relatives who had lost dear ones in the terrible strife, sympathized, if only silently, with the sadness that must accompany their spending of the festival. In this way did the festival differ from preceding ones, and though the bells rang as usual there were fewer in the peal by reason that some of the team had gone to the wars, and although the fine old Christmas hymns were sung in the churches with the same heartiness and feeling, absent well-known faces and fitting references in sermons emphasized that 'such times in England ne'er has been', and gave strength to the hope that they 'ne'er again would be'.

Indeed, the churches and chapels were packed with their usual Christmas worshippers, but it was noticed that the decorations in St John's Church were somewhat muted as it was felt that their usual lavishness would be ill-keeping with the sadness the war had brought to many families.

At the Hospital, only ten of the twenty beds were occupied, but the Matron, Miss Raynor, and the nursing staff ensured that the patients had a 'jolly time'. The two wards were decorated on Christmas morning, each patient received a present, and it was turkey and plum pudding for dinner. In the afternoon, the Revd Tritton, the curate at St John's, conducted a 'bright service', and the day was rounded off 'pleasantly with games'. During the afternoon of Boxing Day, each patient invited two friends to a celebration around the Christmas tree set up for the day, and the main event in the evening was 'the investigation of the mysteries of the interior of a huge snow ball and this revealed such a wealth of treasure that all present were made happy with a gift, even Rob the Hospital dog received a parcel containing an extra succulent bone.

All the Union Poor Law Workhouses across the country had now been renamed by Government Order, 'The Institution', and at The Institution on Preston Road, the usual Christmas celebrations proceeded unaffected by the war. The main event of Christmas Day was the great dinner of roast beef, vegetables, pudding, sweets, cider, mineral waters and coffee. The concert which followed the afternoon service conducted by the Institution's chaplain, the Revd Jenkyns, Rector of Barwick, was presided over by the Master, Mr F. W. Wilton in the 'brilliantly decorated dinning hall'. Songs were sung, piano pieces played and 'an amusing play was presented by the officers entitled 'Mrs Baxter's Baby' '.

The Post Office was as busy as usual with the heavy Christmas mail, and the pressure was greater than normally expected by the late running of some of the mail trains arising from the large-scale movement of troops and war munitions. Also, the postal staff had been depleted by the loss of regular postmen to the military, and the difficulty in recruiting suitable temporary replacements. However, the household deliveries were on time and the Christmas morning delivery was completed. At Christmas 1914, there

Medical and nursing staff of Yeovil Hospital in 1914.

were over 50 sub-post offices in the Yeovil district.

On 28 December 1914, Sapper D. A. Jones of the Royal Engineers wrote home:

> I hope you enjoyed yourselves at Christmas. We had a decent time under the circumstances. The weather was absolutely great on Christmas and Boxing-days. Christmas morning we had a game of football to get us in form for our dinner which we put away in great style. The Christmas pudding etc. was a treat. I am sending you my gift from Princess Mary, as I think it will be worth keeping, also the Christmas card from the King and Queen. The tie pin was given me by a French artilleryman. Things are a bit different this Christmas, but we still enjoy ourselves, and I never thought for a moment we should have had such a decent time.

After two years service in the Royal Engineers on the Western Front, Sapper Douglas Arthur Jones, was badly wounded, lost his right eye and was invalided out of the army in June 1917. Sadly as a result of the wounds and sickness, Douglas Jones died on 23 August 1917 in his parents' home at Brunswick Street, and was laid to rest in Yeovil Cemetery with full military honours. He was twenty-four years old.

No 1 Platoon, D Company, (Yeovil), 2nd Battalion, Somerset Volunteer Regiment at Barwick Park.

VOLUNTEER TRAINING CORPS

Behind the Regular, New and Territorial Armies at the outbreak of War in August 1914, there was a large number of men debarred by age, occupation or medical conditions, from serving in the armed forces but who were keen to carryout some active duty at home.

Movements for home defence sprang up across the country bearing such names as Home Guards, Home Defence Leagues, Citizens' Corps and such like, and who with the help of old soldiers of all ranks and other trained men, quickly grew into companies and battalions.

By November 1914, a Central Association of Volunteer Training Corps had been formed but despite the War Office's recognition of the Association as a properly constituted organization, the new Volunteer Training Battalions were not. As a consequence the volunteer companies and battalions had to be self-financing, the members to provide and pay for uniforms which had to be completely distinguishable both in colour and design from that of the Army; military khaki was forbidden and the majority of the volunteers' uniforms would be lovatt green. All volunteers had to wear a War Office red armband bearing the letters 'GR' for *Georgius Rex*. Because of the shortage of rifles and other equipment for the fighting services, none were issued for some time and many units depended upon private firearms for shooting practice; dummy firearms were used for drill.

Despite the widespread formation of volunteer battalions it appeared that they had no legal status until in July 1915 it was discovered that the Volunteer Act 1863 which authorized the establishment of volunteer regiments was still in force. The battalions of the Volunteer Training Corps were re-enrolled as Volunteer Regiments and would become 'Volunteer Battalions' of the local Regiment.

With the final recognition of the Volunteer Training Corps, rifles and machine guns were issued, and with the increased military training and experience gained by the volunteers, the new battalions became an efficient and proficient home defence force. In the event of invasion, the battalions would guard and defend lines of communication, guard vulnerable areas, man defensive lines and garrison major towns. They also carried out day-to-day duties, providing guards for railway stations, helping with the harvest, transporting wounded soldiers, fire fighting and other assistance when requested by the civil authority.

With the cessation of hostilities in November 1918, the Volunteer Battalions were stood down, and officially disbanded in January 1920.

On Wednesday, 17 September 1914, Yeovil Town Hall was filled to capacity with an enthusiastic audience eager to form a volunteer force open to all men who were not eligible to join the Army. The Mayor, Councillor Norman Buchanan, was in the chair, and after a long and noisy discussion, it was unanimously agreed to establish a company or companies to be named The Athletes' Volunteer Force. (Why 'Athletes'? History remains silent).

On the following Monday over 100 men and youths attended the first parade of the AVF held in the Corn Exchange next to the town hall when two companies were formed. 'A' company for men over the military age of thirty-five or those between nineteen and thirty-three who had been refused enlistment on medical grounds and 'B' company for those between sixteen and nineteen who were too young to join up. Forming up behind the Yeovil Town Band and under the joint command of Dr Haig and Mr E. R. Chaffey, the two companies marched through the main streets to Stoford and back though Newton Park.

The first orders were to parade for Squad Drill in the Corn Exchange at 2.30 p.m. on Saturday 26 September and march to the Pen Mill Football Ground (next to the Pen Mill Hotel).

During the following weeks the Athletes' drilled and route marched, and the use of the Territorial Drill Hall at Southville was granted for drills and target practice on the miniature rifle range. Subscriptions were started for running expenses, a number of rifles were loaned and there were gifts of ammunition.

By April 1915, the AVF had affiliated to the Central Association, and was re-titled Volunteer Training Corps (Yeovil Unit) with one company of two platoons. The officers and NCOs were elected and an 'old and experienced officer', Lieutenant Colonel C. V. Yates, was elected commander. During the summer of 1915, the company trained, drilled, shot and carried out regular field exercises on Babylon Hill, Newton Farm and Barwick Park. Until October the volunteers had worn their civilian clothes with the official red armband but on Sunday 31 October, they formed up in new grey green uniforms at church parade outside St John's in 'a downpour of rain'.

Many of the young Volunteers joined the Army when they were old enough and nineteen-year-old Jack Chudleigh was one. He would win the Military Medal whilst serving with the London Scottish, but would be killed on the Somme in September 1916.

The close of 1916 saw the Yeovil unit of the Volunteer Training Corps become D Company of the 2nd Battalion Somerset Volunteer Regiment and in April 1917 the company was transferred to the 3rd Battalion. The Yeovil volunteers were now very well trained in the use of rifles and machine guns, expert in digging trenches and field work and the company officers and NCOs were attending training courses with the regular Army.

The end came in 1919 when the Somerset Volunteer Battalions were disbanded quietly and like the old saying about old soldiers they just faded away.

'BLACK OUT'

From the early months of the War, there was concern that the Germans might carryout some form of attack from the air. In December 1914, Scarborough, Hartlepool and Whitby were bombarded from the sea by an element of the German High Seas Fleet, and in January 1915, two German Zeppelin airships bombed King's Lynn and Great Yarmouth. London was bombed by Zeppelins on 31 May 1915 and during the remaining war years, attacks by Zeppelins and later by Gotha bomber aircraft would extend to the Home Counties, Midlands, the East Coast and as far north as Edinburgh. Thankfully, the air raids did not reach the West Country but nevertheless the Government's air raid precautions and lighting regulations were observed and enforced.

On 28 January 1915 Yeovil Borough Council took precautionary measures in case of attack from enemy aircraft by reducing the street lighting to alternate lamps and these were to be shaded on the tops. The lighting of the Town Hall clock was discontinued, and picture palace proprietors, shopkeepers and other businesses were required to extinguish their outside lights at 7 p.m. On the receipt of a warning of the approach of enemy aircraft, the Gas Works' hooter would sound a series of long blasts with intermittent sharp blasts and similar warnings would be sounded on the factory hooters of Messrs Petters' Nautilus Works in Reckleford, Messrs Whitby's glove factory behind Middle Street, Messrs Aplin & Barrett's Newton Road Creamery and Brutton's Brewery at Clarence Street.

However, in June 1915 the Government relaxed the regulations and only places around the coast were subject to lighting restrictions, but following the air raids on London the regulations were revived.

In March 1916 the Borough Council was informed that the Yeovil police had introduced a new procedure to be carried out on receipt of an air raid warning. Constables and Special constables would go to the parts of the town allocated to them, turn off all the street lamps and warn householders to turn off lights. In the case of fire, the Fire Brigade would be mustered and the Ambulance Corps would be

A German Zeppelin raider is shot down over Essex on 24 September 1916.

placed on stand-by. The Special constables were being trained and handbills distributed explaining the procedures.

In April, the Home Office issued instructions to local councils to restrict public lighting to street corners only and in compliance, the Council reduced the burners in each lamp to one, turned off the light of the Town Hall clock and also the light in the recently erected turret clock on the Central Junior School. All commercial and domestic lights had to be obscured by curtains or blinds but it was agreed to keep lit the lamp outside the police station at Union Street to help people in the event of emergencies.

The Government's regulation also required all vehicles to provide a red rear light lit after dark and believe it or not, hand carts and push chairs had to have lights! On 1 August 1916, Henry Bartholomew was fined one shilling for wheeling an unlit pair of hand trucks and on 26 September, Mary Warner of Smith's Terrace was fined one shilling for 'wheeling a push-chair without a light'; it was an offence to push a bicycle after dark without a lit rear red light.

On 24 November the *Western Gazette* suggested to readers that, 'As lighting regulations keep the streets of the town in darkness it would avoid many unpleasant experiences if pedestrians would observe the rule of walking on the right side of the road or pavement.'

On December 15, grocers Messrs C. J. Hook & Sons of the Golden Canister, Middle Street, announced in the *Gazette* that 'Owing to the Restricted Lighting Conditions we are not displaying our usual elaborate window show of Christmas Specialities', but in the 'well-lit showroom' all customers could inspect the Christmas fare in comfort.

The lighting restrictions continued through 1917 and on 8 October, the Borough Surveyor informed the Council that the lower parts of the lampposts, curb stones and steps had been painted white to assist the public during the dark winter nights. By early 1918, because it was most unlikely that the town would suffer an air raid, the lighting restrictions were eased but because of the acute coal shortage the Council decided that no street lamps would be lit during the summer months.

Following the cessation of hostilities in November, the regulations lapsed, but due to the continuing severe coal shortage the Borough Council decided to restrict the winter lighting to twenty-one lamps.

1915

THE RED CROSS MILITARY HOSPITAL

There is a plaque on the outside wall of Pegasus Court (former Newnam Memorial Hall) facing South Street, which commemorates the use of the Hall as a Red Cross Military Hospital during the First World War.

The horrendously high casualties being suffered by the Army on the Western Front was placing a tremendous strain on the nation's civilian and military hospitals and to meet this challenge public halls, large houses, schools and many other buildings, both public and private, were being adapted to treat the thousands of wounded men.

In January 1915, the Trustees of the South Street Baptist School, granted the British Red Cross Society the free use of the Newnam Memorial Hall for a sixty-two-bed auxiliary military hospital, and by the time the last wounded soldier left in December 1918, some 1,200 men had been nursed back to health.

The hospital comprised four wards, a well-equipped operating theatre, a recreation and dining room, bathroom, Commandant's room, kitchen and stores. An X-ray apparatus, purchased by voluntary contributions, was operated in the Nursing Home at Kingston Manor, which in 1922 would become part of the new Yeovil District Hospital. Three motor ambulances were used for the transport of casualties, one purchased with the aid of private donations, one loaned by Messrs White Bros, house furnishers, and a third the gift of members of the Ivel Club and Mr W. H. Hine. Nursing was carried out by a small trained staff of Sisters and Red Cross Nurses supervised by the full-time Commandant Mrs L. K. Stobart, and assisted by volunteers from the Somerset/80 (Women) and Somerset/19 (Men) Voluntary Aid Detachments (VAD), the latter undertaking night duties as well transporting the casualties; local surgeons and physicians also gave their services.

The first patients were men serving with the Army Service Corps and Territorial units temporarily billeted in Yeovil and of the 103 were treated, only one, Private Ernest Baker, died in April.

In July 1915 the hospital was recognised as a Primary Station and immediately

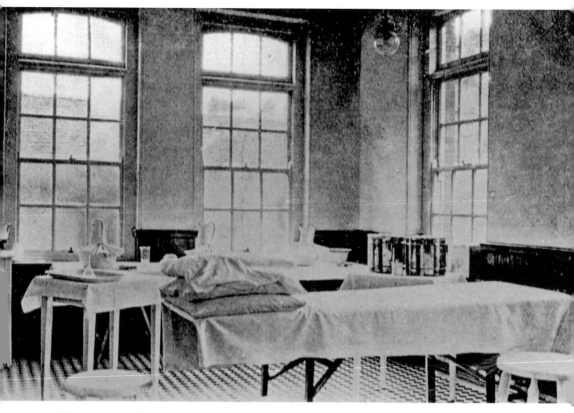

The operating theatre in the Red Cross Military Hospital.

began to receive men from the various battle Fronts. The wounded were brought straight from the hospital ships to Sherborne railway station, the designated place of detrainment, and transported to Yeovil in motor ambulances driven and manned by members of the Men's VAD.

Although many of the men were very ill when they arrived, only four died out of the 1,200 treated, which reflected great credit on the skill and dedication of the medical and nursing staff.

The hospital was never short of support from the townspeople who provided funds, hospitality and entertainment for the men, and a working party of local lady volunteers, assisted in mending the hospital and the men's equipment and another band of volunteers helped in the kitchen.

During the four years the sum of £4,000 was received in voluntary gifts from the Yeovil area and £9,000 spent on running the Hospital.

Shortly before the Hospital closed in December 1918, the County Director of the British Red Cross Society told a gathering of organisations which had helped with the running of the hospital, that the Society fully acknowledged the magnificent loyalty and sacrifice of all the workers and no words could express all that the men owed to their unfailing service and their splendid spirit throughout the many trying days of the War. The County Director also believed that the presence of the 'boys in blue', wounded servicemen wore light blue jackets and trousers, a white shirt and red tie, 'had made the people of Yeovil better citizens'.

YEOVIL VOLUNTARY AID DETACHMENTS

In 1909 Voluntary Aid Detachments, the VADs were set up by the British Red Cross Society and the Order of St John of Jerusalem to provide medical services to the newly- formed Territorial Medical Service.

The VADs were organised into county branches with local volunteers, both women and men, trained in first aid and nursing. When War broke out in 1914, the VADs combined under the British Red Cross, and organised the establishment of the auxiliary military hospitals throughout the country with members carrying on a wide range of duties from general nursing to transport services.

In the previous chapter I described the Red Cross Military Hospital set up in the Newnam Memorial Hall by the two Yeovil Voluntary Aid Detachments, the Somerset /80 (Women), Commandant Mrs L. K. Stobart, and the Somerset/19 (Men) commanded by Lieutenant Colonel C. J. Trask.

The nursing of the wounded and the sick soldier patients was carried out by full-time Nursing Sisters under the Superintendent, Miss Hodges, assisted by lady

Members of the Somerset/19 (Men) Voluntary Aid Detachment.

volunteers and the Men's Detachment provided transport and night orderly duties.

On 27 August 1915, the *Western Gazette* described the arrival of wounded soldiers from the Western Front and how they were received by the VADs.

Sherborne, being the centre for the hospitals of Yeovil, Wincanton, Compton, Yetminster and Chetnole, the hospital train which has brought the men brought from a hospital ship putting in to a certain port [censorship forbad the naming of the port] discharges there. On Tuesday, the news that a train would arrive that morning was only received in Sherborne and Yeovil a couple of hours before the time fixed for the arrival, and at once the excellent organisation of the VADs goes to work. Motor-cars, motor-cycles and other messengers dash round and warn owners of motor-cars of all descriptions, and the stretcher bearers of the detachment, who at once leave businesses and occupations, and, in the case of the Yeovil contingent, report at the Hospital in South Street. Cars and orderlies are dispatched to Sherborne Station and the messengers are directed towards calling out members of the VTC [Volunteer Training Corps] who later assemble and clear a space at the Hospital in which the cars may unload.

The time fixed for the arrival of the train is 12.15, and soon the roadway in front of Sherborne Station is filled with cars, whilst on the up-platform the VAD men go about their duties with an absence of fuss and confusion which denotes a knowledge of their business as accurate as the dressing of the grim line of stretchers laid out in readiness on the platform. The men are mustered, Sherborne and Yeovil members shoulder to shoulder and Commandant, Mr F. Trevett, of Sherborne, and Dr H. R. Unwin of Yeovil, satisfy themselves that all is ready. At the exact time, the hospital train runs through on the down line to shunt back to the up-platform to discharge its burden, and as it slows up, windows and open doors are filled with the bronzed faces of the men who are able to move about. On board there are about 170 cases, 'none really bad, ' says an orderly at an open door, and it would be hard to image anything more comfortable than a glimpse inside the train discloses. The heavy London and North Western Railway cars have been transformed into spotlessly clean and airy wards, and there is a kitchen car and other cars for some of the staff. Chalked on a panel of one car is '13 cot cases ' and inside on trim little cots lie the wounded, cheery optimists to a man, whose hurts forbid their walking. A laughing private of the West Kents is coming back after a year of war, glad he is to get home and a companion on the other side of the gangway says that the arrangements for the wounded could not be better, and they have had a most comfortable journey.

After some delay caused by the train having to pull back to a siding to allow the passage of the up train, the work is proceeded with. Gangways are put out from the cars, and the wounded who can walk are then told off to the waiting motor-cars and quickly taken to their allotted hospitals which are indicated by a label attached to their jackets. Meanwhile, the stretcher-bearers carry their loads firmly and gently to the waiting motor ambulances, and the injured soldiers are driven carefully to their destinations.

That all the injuries are not the direct outcome of contact with the weapons of war is instanced by the case of a much bandaged private of the Royal Berkshires, who escaped unscathed amid all the dangers of the great retreat from Mons, the onslaughts at the Marne, and some winter trench work at La Basse, to meet with a violent spill from a cycle into shell hole on a very dark road thus badly injuring his shoulder.

When the VAD men have placed their charges in hospital, much work lies before them in detail duty at the institution plus turns at night duty all the times the building is occupied. For the most part they are men of non-military age or with sufficient reasons for not joining the Army. They have put in hours of training, and that they have worked to some purpose and are really an effective body doing much excellent service in an unobtrusive manner, is evident to anyone able to watch them at their work of mercy when the battered and maimed warriors reach home again from those indeterminate areas known as 'the Front '.

APRIL

Yeovil in April 1915 was in the midst of a measles epidemic, and all the schools had been closed from mid-March until the end of the Easter holidays on 12 April. The town Medical Officer of Health advised the Education Committee at the end of March that he hoped the epidemic would more or less be over by the middle of April.

More worryingly, the Medical Officer warned the town authorities that there was a serious outbreak of smallpox in Bristol, and all precautions should be taken to ensure that the dreaded disease did not break out in Yeovil. Thankfully this did not happen and the town escaped infection.

Looking through the *Western Gazette's* Yeovil News columns of April 1915, there seem to be few reports to raise the spirits of the readers. Entertainments were either few or not being reported, which was unlikely. However, there were some whist drives; a team from glove manufacturers, Messrs Blake & Co. met a team from the locally billeted Army Service Corps and drew fifteen games each, a great surprise because the glovers were the Yeovil Whist League champions! There was a large participation of over 200 players in the second whist drive to raise funds for the Red Cross Military Hospital, held at the Skating Rink in Hendford (opposite the Manor Hotel). During the evening, the Yeovil Whist League Shield was presented to the champions, the team from Messrs Blake & Co. and the 'wooden spoon' to the Ivel Club team.

Long's Restaurant was the venue for a whist drive between St Ivel and B Section of the Army Service Corps on 6 April and the local team narrowly beat the military by fifteen games to fourteen. A musical programme followed the whist presented by Messrs Burgess, Chubb, Maughan, Rivers, Vincent, Lance-Corporal George and Driver Smith.

Some ninety dancers enjoyed a 'long-night' dance in the Skating Rink on Easter Monday, 5 April to music by Messrs Harbour and Harvey on the piano and violin. The proceeds were given to the Tobacco Fund for the men of the Somerset Light Infantry stationed in India.

Buses waiting in Lower Middle Street to be driven off for conversion into ambulances for the Western Front.

A concert in aid of the Serbian Relief Fund was held at the Princes Street Assembly Rooms on 26 April, and the large audience enjoyed a varied programme of violin solos, duets at the piano, recitations and classical and English dances performed by Mrs Twycrosse's Dance Academy. The audience joined in lustily with national and patriotic songs, and the finale was a representative tableau of 'The Allies'.

Sadly, the telegrams continued to arrive as another family lost a father, brother, son or friend on one of the battlefronts. Mr F. Ashley of 20 Everton Road, received the dreaded telegram telling him that his brother Corporal C. Y. Ashley had been killed in action on the Western Front. The widowed Mrs Hayward of 53 Huish, learnt that her son Stanley, who was serving in the Royal Field Artillery, had died on 10 April at the Isle of Wight Red Cross Hospital from enteric fever contracted during treatment for a severe head injury received when playing hockey.

The first death occurred at the Red Cross Military Hospital in the Newnam Memorial Hall, South Street on 16 April when Private Ernest Baker of the 5th Battalion, Somerset Light Infantry, temporarily billeted in the town, died from pneumonia and bronchitis. Private Baker left a widow and seven young children and was buried with full military honours at Taunton.

All the previous deaths were great tragedies for the families and friends, but the one which I found in the columns of the *Western Gazette* is perhaps even sadder, and relates to the death of eight-year-old Ivy Hamblin.

During the early evening of 12 April, Mr Fred Clements of The Park, drove his motor car down Reckleford and as he turned into Earle Street, he could see three young girls standing on the right-hand pavement about 50 yards along the street. Suddenly one of the girls ran backwards across the road in front of him waving a skipping rope over her head. Mr Clements swung the car hard to the left, sounded the horn, shouted a warning and slammed on the brakes. Although the motor had slowed to less than a walking pace the offside front wing struck the child and knocked her down. Corporal Charles Yeo of the 4th Dorsets, was standing chatting to Walter Vose at the corner of Reckleford and Earle Street and took little notice of the passing motor car until he heard the sound of a horn and a man shouting. Turning to see what the commotion was all about, he saw a young girl running backwards across the street waving a skipping rope over her head. Charles saw the car swerve to the left and was horrified to see the right wing strike her and the front wheel roll over the child. The two friends ran to give assistance and moved the unconscious little girl from under the vehicle. The child was identified as Ivy Hamblin who lived in Reckleford and she was gently lifted into the car and driven to the Yeovil Hospital by a very distressed and shocked Mr Fred Clements. Sadly Ivy died on the way to the hospital and although on examination there were no external signs of injury she had suffered severe internal injuries. Three of her right ribs were broken and the end of one had been driven into her lung and damaged the liver. The child had died from a massive internal hemorrhage.

At the inquest, the events leading up to the accident were recounted and eleven-year-old Gwen Rowsell stated that she was standing with her sister Dorothy talking to Ivy when suddenly she ran backwards across the street. Gwen had not been aware of the approach of the motor car until she heard the horn and the shouting and turning around saw Ivy knocked down.

Following evidence of the cause of death given by Dr Unwin, the coroner summed up by stating that he did not consider any blame could be attached to Mr Clements and the jury returned the verdict that Ivy Hamblin had died from injuries caused by her having been knocked down by a motor car and no blame could be attributed to anyone.

Meanwhile across the English Channel on 22 April 1915, the first successful lethal chlorine poison gas attack was carried out by the Germans at Ypres.

THE STORY OF WESTLAND AIRCRAFT

The story of Westland Aircraft (now Augusta/Westland) from its beginnings in 1915 has been thoroughly covered by a number of authors over the years, but the following article was written by one of the founding members and first Chairman of the firm, Sir Ernest W. Petter, and published in the first edition of the *Yeovil Review* in October 1936.

Twenty-one years ago last April, three men walked down to the corner of a field just outside Yeovil, where there was a small farm hut. One of the three, the only

The Westland Works expanded rapidly from the early beginnings in April 1915.

survivor, and the author of this little story, opened the door of the hut and solemnly said: 'This is the Westland Aircraft Works.'

The circumstances that led up to this incident were as follows. Mr Lloyd George a few days previously, it being the second year of the war, had made in Parliament a very serious speech, in which he frankly exposed the inadequacy and unsuitability of the munitions available for carrying on the war.

The writer hastily convened a Board Meeting of Petters Limited, then a comparatively small Company manufacturing oil engines, and the Board passed a resolution by which they placed at the disposal of the Government the whole of their manufacturing resources, to make anything or everything the Government might call for from them. A copy of this resolution was on the same day sent to the War Office and the Admiralty. From the former nothing was heard but almost the next day a telegram came from the Admiralty asking that two representatives might go up for conference. The writer accompanied by his brother, Mr P. W. Petter, accordingly went to London and were received by five gentlemen, at least three of whom were Lords of the Admiralty, who stated that the great need of the Navy was seaplanes, and were we willing to make them.

We explained that our experience and factory were not exactly in line with their requirements, but we were willing to attempt anything which would help the Country. 'Good,' said they, 'you are the fellows we want; we will send you the drawings and give you all the help we can. Get on with it.'

So we got on with it, and before the end of the war the little hut in the corner of the field became a great factory, in which, when the armistice was declared in 1918, 1,100 aeroplanes had been turned out. A telegram received from the Ministry of Munitions after the armistice, testified to the appreciation of the Westland effort and the satisfaction given by the excellence of the machines turned out, which, from the first, had secured a great reputation for reliability and quality of the manufacture, under the guidance of Mr R. A. Bruce, who very early in the venture took charge of the Department and remained with the Company until 1934.

The DH9A machines, which became after the second year our principal product, were two-seater machines, and every aeroplane was sent over to Dunkerque the same day as it was completed and tested. One pilot flew it across and it was therefore necessary to provide balast to compensate for the empty seat.

A brainy individual discovered that a twelve-gallon cask of cider for which the Yeovil neighbourhood is famous was just the right weight, and this was therefore adopted as the correct ballast for a DH9A and used accordingly. Many an airman has told me of the joy with which the Westland DH9A's were welcomed in France, and the double comfort each machine brought in added fighting power, and the good stuff that accompanied it.

CALEB NEWIS

One of the first Yeovilians to volunteer for the new Kitchener's Army was thirty-two-year-old Caleb Newis, who in partnership with his younger brother Albert, had succeeded their father in the business of millers and corn merchants in Preston Road. The mill, known for many years as Newis's Mill, stood at what is now the entrance to Willow Road from Preston Road.

Caleb was said to have been an excellent marksman and had served in the cyclist section of F Company, 2nd Volunteer Battalion, Somerset Light Infantry until it was disbanded on the formation of the new Territorial Army in 1908. He subsequently served with D Squadron, West Somerset Yeomanry and was a member of the Yeovil Company of the National Reserve.

On the outbreak of war, Caleb with other members of the National Reserve, joined the New Army 6th (Service) Battalion of the Somerset Light Infantry, which when it left for the Western Front in May 1915 was described as 'a fine Battalion with a high state of efficiency, worthy to take its place alongside those splendid Regular Battalions which had gone before them'.

Three of Caleb's letters home were published in the *Western Gazette* and the first appeared in the edition of 9 July, some two months after the battalion had left for the Front:

> We marched fourteen miles and then went into the trenches in the fighting line and a rather warm corner near a place that is absolutely smashed. It is indescribable. The trenches occupied by our Battalion were in some places only about 14 yards from the Germans and they kept reminding us with a few shells. We were on practically all the

Caleb Edney Newis.

time with very little rest. I am sorry to say that we have had a great many casualties, and since our arrival we have lost about 60 officers and men including the captain of our Company and also a lieutenant. We are very sorry as they were very decent fellows but, am pleased to say they are only wounded. Our regimental sergeant-major, who has been with us ever since the first day at Taunton was killed on Monday, and he will be sadly missed. Two or three others I know well have been killed and some have nasty wounds, but a good many only slightly. It was a case of when you were standing up and heard a shell coming 'bobbing down' or throwing yourself down on the ground. I think the less I tell you about our five days there the better, as some things would be rather gruesome… I think we were all rather glad to get away for a day or two as it seemed to get on one's nerves a little. They gave us a lively time on Monday night; it simply rained shells for 20 minutes. They fell in hundreds but did not do a lot of damage. The 'Yeovil Boys' are all fairly well bar Salter who had a slight shrapnel wound on the thumb but nothing serious. He has gone to hospital somewhere.

The writer expresses himself as being well supplied with tobacco and cigarettes in common with the regiment, and says that he has just received two tins of tobacco and a packet of cigarettes, part of a parcel from several well-known Yeovil men he mentions. He says it is very kind of them and the Yeovil men greatly appreciate the gift and shows they are thinking of them.

In August Caleb was wounded by shrapnel in the left shoulder and right knee which he wrote as being 'very slight' and on the 13th the *Gazette* published extracts from his letter describing what happened next:

Till anyone is wounded it is impossible for them to know the kindness of the RAMC. After being wounded a man is temporarily dressed by one of his comrades or a stretcher bearer and then waits for the opportunity to be taken to the Battalion's dressing-station. Then he is taken over by the RAMC to the clearing station and is then sent off to the hospital. He is supplied with hot cocoa and bread and butter and with cocoa and ham sandwiches during the journey which in my case lasted about seven hours. The wounded were there taken off by motor to the camp. I can assure you that after being the trenches for twelve days, I enjoyed a nice bath and a complete change of clothes, and a nice clean white bed. We are looked after admirably, the sisters being only too pleased to do anything for us. There are three of us from Yeovil who are wounded – E. Bragg, Gerrard and myself.

The next letter appeared in the *Western Gazette* on 10 March 1916.

Lance-Corporal C. E. Newis, of the 6th Somersets, in a letter home gives an interesting account of a meeting of the 1st and 6th Somerset Battalions. He says:- 'A few days ago while we were marching through a French village a very pleasant little incident occurred. We happened to meet for the first time being in this country, the 1st Battalion, who were billeted there. We didn't stop but went on to another village, but the next day were allowed to visit the 1st, and also the day after. I met many well-known to me, including Sergeant Boucher (son of Mr Boucher of Bradford Abbas), Lance-Corporal Pippard (son of Mr Pippard, Watercombe, Preston) Private Beaton, Hellier, Cooper, Gundry (of Yeovil) and a good many others. Our band paid a visit to the village on the second afternoon. In every estaminet, you could see old chums having a drink in celebration of the occasion and a most enjoyable time was spent. But on the third day we received marching orders and have left them a few miles away, being on our way to the trenches once more. They all looked remarkably well and fit.

Sadly the next time we read about Caleb Newis is on 29 September 1916 when the *Western Gazette* reports that:

Official intimation has been received by the relatives of Lance Corporal C. E. Newis, of Preston Road, that he has been missing since an attack on September 16th. The letter also received from the adjutant of his Battalion, after enquiries made amongst the men of his platoon, says that he can give no further information than that contained in the official notification.

The *Western Gazette*, 3 November 1916:

Notification was received on Monday morning that Lance Corporal C. E. Newis, elder son of the late Mr J. H. Newis and Mrs Newis of Preston Road, was killed in action on September 16th. He was 34 years of age, and leaves a widow and two young children, [Dorothy and Marion] with whom the utmost sympathy has been expressed.

The *Western Gazette*, 10 November 1916:

The Union Jack was hung on the pulpit at the Vicarage Street Wesleyan Church on Sunday in memory of the late Corporal C. E. Newis of the Somerset Light Infantry. Special reference was made by the Revd W. M. J. Noble, to Corporal Newis's death, he being a member of the congregation, and had passed through all the classes of the Sunday School. Sympathy was also expressed with the relatives.

Caleb Newis served with the 6th Battalion through some of the fiercest fighting on the Western Front, including the Battles of the Somme, but he has no known grave and his name is recorded on the Thiepval Memorial to the missing Pier and Face 2A.

AUGUST

July 1915 had been a very wet month in Yeovil but August Bank Holiday Monday, 2 August, was described by the *Western Gazette* as 'probably the quietest and most unpleasant ever experienced, certainly for many years, for rain descended practically incessantly throughout the day'. From early morning until late that evening, the rain pelted down and few ventured out of doors to enjoy the holiday except those rushing to catch the excursion train at Pen Mill station to enjoy a wet day at Weymouth and the coast.

A 'patriotic fête' in aid of the Red Cross Military Hospital and Patriotic Fund had been organized for Bank Holiday Monday at Newton Park and several thousand people from Yeovil and district had bought admission tickets in advance. At half-past eight on Monday morning the Fête Committee met and decided to go ahead despite the weather so that 'country people' would not be disappointed, and in the hope that the rain would stop before midday when the gates opened. However, the torrential downpour showed no signs of letting up and at half-past ten the Committee met again and decided it was hopeless to continue, and postponed the fête until the coming Saturday 7 August; all advance paid tickets would be valid on Saturday.

Happily, Saturday turned out warm and sunny and remained so all day, typical!! Over 6,000 people enjoyed a programme of athletic sports and in the adjoining River Yeo, swimming races and diving. There were side shows, comic football, skittles for a live pig, races for soldiers and sailors in uniform, musical chairs, wheelbarrow and obstacle races, all for quite reasonable cash prizes (except for the skittles). There was

Enjoying a charabanc trip to the seaside.

a small pleasure fair and a 'telegraph office' from which a message could be delivered to anyone in the Park for a penny. During the evening a variety concert was given at Newton House and there was dancing in a large marquee to the music of the Sherborne Military Band. The Committee deemed the postponed fête a great success.

The weather, however, had not finished with Yeovil, when one week later on Saturday morning, 14 August, a succession of 'terrific thunderstorms' broke over the town at about 11 o'clock. The storms rattled on for several hours, turning streets into rivers and flooding much of the lower parts of the town. Thankfully there were no reports of lightning or flood damage to buildings, but many standing crops in the fields around Yeovil were badly beaten down by the torrential rain. There was another two hours downpour three days later, but with no thunder or lightning. Once again the lower parts of the town were flooded, and thankfully all buildings escaped the torrents.

Bad weather did not spoil the trip by Borough Councillors and officials in a motor charabanc to view the sources of the town's water supply at Spring Pond, near Evershot, where a picnic lunch was enjoyed. After lunch the party were driven to the Haydon Wood spring where they were met by the Town Clerk, Major H. C. Batten, home on leave recuperating from the effects of gas poisoning, and who gave 'an interesting account of his time in the firing-line'.

Likewise the weather smiled kindly on 'outings' enjoyed by the employees of glove manufacturers, Messrs Thring and Luffman by motor charabanc to Cheddar and on to Weston-super-Mare for dinner, and the ladies of glove manufacturers, Messrs Ewens and Johnson enjoyed a similar trip to Cheddar and Weston-super-Mare.

During August, the *Western Gazette* was advertising for 'A Respectable, Intelligent Lad (about 14) WANTED in the Reading Room', but six young lads aged nine to thirteen years old would certainly not have fallen into the 'Respectable' category.

The six 'boys' from Huish appeared before the Children's Court charged with destroying crops of apples and plums growing in the West Hendford garden of Mr Frederick Cole, the proprietor of the Three Choughs Hotel (now Becket House). Mr Cole told the court that one plum tree had been completely stripped of fruit, apple trees had been damaged, and a basket load of potatoes strewn about. The sow, which he kept in a sty in the garden, had been released and had eaten over 200 celery plants and lettuces. There had been damage on four recent occasions, and vegetables and fruit stolen. The boys before the court had been seen in the garden and reported to the police.

All six pleaded guilty, the two oldest were each sentenced to receive six strokes of the birch, their parents fined five shillings (weekly wages averaged between £1 and £2), and the younger four to receive three strokes each and their parents fined two shillings and six pence.

Five police constables from the Yeovil Division of the County Constabulary were released at their request to join the army. PC Stevens enlisted in the Army Mounted Police, PCs Powis, Jackson and Furnimere in the Army Foot Police and PC Miller to be a shoeing smith in the Army Service Corps.

Two Yeovil public officials serving on the Western Front were reported to have been wounded.

Councillor Ernest Farr, a veteran of the Boer War and a member of the National Reserve, and now a sergeant in the 6th Battalion, Somerset Light Infantry, had been badly wounded by shrapnel. Councillor Farr would be medically discharged on account of his wounds, would return to take up his seat on the Borough Council and be elected Mayor for 1921/22

The second was Corporal Fenwick, another National Reservist serving with the Somerset Light Infantry's 6th Battalion, who was wounded by shrapnel; Corporal Fenwick had been the assistant manager of the Town Gas Works. He would recover from his wounds and eventually return to his old job.

UP BEFORE THE BENCH

During the war years, local magistrates had to deal with many cases which would not have come before the Bench in more peaceful times.

One of the regulars was dealing with soldiers absent from their units. All soldiers and sailors would carry a pay book as their means of identification and a pass if they were on leave. The police were authorized to demand the production of identification and if this could not be presented or a leave pass shown, the serviceman would be arrested, brought before the magistrates to await the return to his unit or ship under military escort. The cases which came before the Yeovil magistrates are too numerous to describe, but the following will give some idea of those which the Bench dealt with during the Great War.

Private William Torry of the 3rd Battalion, Somerset Light Infantry stationed in Crown Hill Barracks at Plymouth was brought up before the Bench on 31 August 1915, charged with being absent from the battalion and was ordered to be handed over to a military court.

Absentees from British regiments were not the only ones to come before the magistrates. Thousands of Australian, New Zealand and Canadian troops were stationed in the south and west of England, but I can find no case of New Zealanders or Canadians being hauled up before the Bench. However, quite a few Australians appeared, probably because many battalions were present in the area for most of the war.

Three Australian private soldiers serving with the 12th Battalion, Australian Force, Fred Scott, Sidney Barclay and Henry Storr appeared on 22 August 1918, for being absent without leave and were remained to await escort back to whatever punishment awaited them.

One quite remarkable case came before the Yeovil Bench on Tuesday 21 December 1915. Private Tom Hillier of the 2nd Battalion, Dorset Regiment, was charged with being a deserter from the Greek city of Salonika, now Thessalonica! Police Constable Seymour testified that acting on information received the previous morning he had gone to the soldier's home in Stoke-sub-Hamdon and asked his mother whether Tom was there. Mrs Hillier confirmed that he was upstairs in bed and on being called down the prisoner stated that he had no leave pass and had deserted.

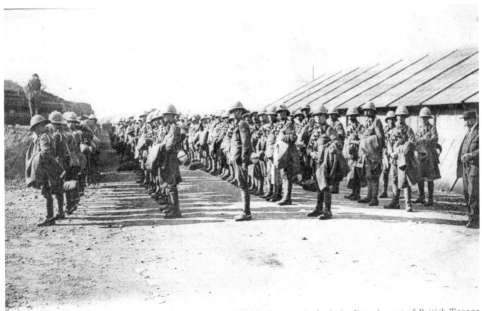

492 Camp Anglais - Arrivée d'un contingent — British Camp - Arrival of a Detachment of British Troops

British troops arrive at the Salonika Front from which Tom Hillier deserted.

Tom Hillier admitted to the magistrates that he was a deserter and stated that he had gone to Salonika with his regiment but had not been there many hours before he deserted. He had no idea why he left the battalion and walked about Salonika but when he tried to rejoin he could not find where it had gone. He went back to the city and changed his clothes with a Greek. After wandering around for a fortnight he got on board a French liner and on reaching Marseilles worked his passage on another boat to Middlesbrough. The sailors on board collected and paid his rail fare to Newport in South Wales, where some friends he visited paid his fare to Langport. He had then walked home to Stoke.

The Bench was informed that the prisoner's battalion had arrived at Salonika in the middle of October and he had joined the Army in Sherborne in November 1914.

The Chairman stated that this was a very serious charge and told Hillier that he would have to return to his regiment and try to make good. He was remanded to await an escort but before being removed from the court, Tom Hillier stated that when he arrived home he expected the police to come for him. His fate remains unknown.

A more common and regular offence brought before and during the war was being drunk and disorderly although in some ways the case of Private Albert Bernas of Queen Street was different. When he appeared before the Bench on 1 September 1917 charged with being drunk that morning, he apologized and stated that he had just arrived home on special leave from twelve months on the Western Front in France. He had met a couple of pals and the two glasses of beer had 'over come him'. The case was dismissed and he promised to behave himself whilst he was home.

The Defence of the Realm legislation required German nationals, no matter how long they had lived in Great Britain, to report and register with the police. Widow Mrs Louisa Egerer and her daughter Violet were living at Ilchester, and both appeared before the magistrates on 16 June 1915, charged with being German nationals and failing to report and register. Both pleaded not guilty.

Yeovil Police Superintendent House told the Bench that his officers had been making enquiries regarding German nationals resident in the area and whilst it was established that Mrs Egerer had been married to a German, neither she nor her daughter had reported or registered.

In her defence Mrs Egerer stated that her late husband had been a commercial traveller, he was a German national, and had died in Brussels in 1889. They had married in London, she had travelled infrequently to Germany but had not been there for at least thirty years. Violet had been born in London in 1874 and apart from spending a short time in Germany when a small child, she had lived all her life in England. In the circumstances neither thought it necessary to report or register as they did not consider they were Germans.

The charge against Violet was withdrawn, but Mrs Egerer was found guilty and fined nine shillings.

Penalties were harsh nearly a century ago and especially on young offenders. For example in December 1916 four young boys, two aged nine and two aged twelve, were charged with stealing cigarettes and an umbrella. On being found guilty the two nine year olds were sentenced to receive four strokes of the birch rod and the twelve year olds to six each.

In June 1916, a 'very bad boy' aged nine was sent to Bath Industrial School until he was sixteen for stealing, damaging property and being 'out all night'. A 'good boy' aged ten was spared the birch for his first offence of stealing a bicycle lamp and the Bench left it to the lad's father to punish him!

RED CROSS DAYS, OCTOBER 1915

In October 1915, the First World War had reached stalemate on the Western Front, and there were no signs of the end to the conflict and carnage.

The British Red Cross Society had selected Friday and Saturday 29 and 30 October as Red Cross Days but this year fund raising would not be confined to selling flags and street collections.

On Saturday afternoon a football match was played on the Pen Mill Athletic Ground between a Yeovil team selected by Mr William Seymour and an Army team from the Wiltshire Royal Engineers stationed at Weymouth. The *Western Gazette* reported that

> The attendance at the football match was not a very large one, but this may be accounted for by the fact that many football enthusiasts in the town have enlisted, and the weather experienced in the afternoon was not at all desirable for spectators. A scratch team was got together in the town to play the Wilts Engineers from Weymouth, whose team it was rumoured contained one or two Swindon professionals. A good game was witnessed, although it was early apparent that Yeovil's unpracticed combination was no match for the burly Engineers, who won by seven goals to one. However, there were no issues at stake.
>
> Mr Plucknett refereed, and the teams were comprised as follows:- Yeovil - Harris; Bowerman and Sims; Larcombe, Maidment and Luffman; Rouse, Versineersich (a Belgian refugee), Hicks, Webb and Elliott. Wilts Engineers - Fisher; Andrews and Arman; Linnett, Hayes and Summers; Lieut. Williams, Covey, Lee, Davies and Mortimer.
>
> Before commencing the teams were lined up and briefly addressed by Colonel W. Marsh (County Director of the Somerset Red Cross Society), who afterwards kicked off.

During the Saturday evening, the local Loyal 'Alexandra' Lodge of Oddfellows organised a concert in the Princes Street Assembly Rooms, with the proceeds of £8 9s going to the British Red Cross Society. Amongst the large audience were a number of nurses and wounded soldiers from the Red Cross Military Hospital. The *Western Gazette* reported that the wounded soldiers thoroughly enjoyed themselves;

> For when not being entertained themselves, they entertained the rest of the audience with some 'tit-bits' of their own, and although when occasionally they did burst into song and harmony was thrown to the winds, their efforts were all the more appreciated as coming from those who had faced the enemy in the service of their country.

The concert programme included 'patriotic airs and a street piano medley', humorous monologues, instrumental pieces, vocals, a musical character sketch 'The Nipper's Lullaby' and at the conclusion, a comic dramatic sketch entitled 'The Domestic Hearthstone or the Maiden's Revenge'.

The two Yeovil Red Cross Days raised over £232 in addition to the £167 already raised for the purchase of a new motor ambulance.

The Wiltshire Royal Engineers' footballers beat a Yeovil team 7-1.

1916

THE YEOVIL ROLL OF HONOUR

The Yeovil Town Hall was packed on Saturday afternoon, 26 February 1916 to witness 'one of the most moving ceremonies that has been witnessed in the Borough for many a day'. The War which so many had predicted would be over by Christmas 1914, was now entering its nineteenth terrible month. In Europe and on battlefields scattered across the world, hundreds of thousands of men and women had lost their lives. The British Regular Army had been virtually wiped out, the Territorial and Kitchener's New Armies were suffering horrendous losses, and the Military Service Act 1916 had just become law introducing national conscription for the first time Great Britain.

Behind a raised platform in the Town Hall, a large Union Jack was hung on one of the walls, and in front of which stood the Mayor, Alderman Edmund Damon, accompanied by members of the Borough Council and other local dignitaries. Addressing the large gathering of townspeople, the Mayor stated that the object of this gathering was to unveil the Yeovil Roll of Honour, and in his opinion the only person entitled to carryout this honourable ceremony was the former Mayoress and widow of the late Mayor, Councillor Norman Buchanan, who had died so tragically following the accident at his home on last New Year's Eve. To warm applause Mrs Norman Buchanan stepped forward and stated that that they must all feel the solemnity of this ceremony to unveil the beautiful picture destined to be Yeovil's Roll of Honour and to have inscribed thereon the names of those who had fallen and those who might be called to yield up their lives during the course of this terrible war. She thought that their feelings must be of sorrow, pride and gratitude; sorrow that there should be the occasion for such a memorial; pride that amidst the tens of thousands of heroes who had nobly given their lives for King and Country, Yeovil men were not wanting; and gratitude for their glorious example and gratitude also the artist who had so patriotically and generously presented this beautiful picture to the town of Yeovil. The list of names to be written on the Roll was getting steadily larger but no matter how they died, from sickness in the training camps, on the field of battle, of wounds, in

The only known surviving image of the painting – The Yeovil Roll of Honour - believed lost in the Town Hall fire in 1935.

hospital, on the high seas as the victims of murderous attacks, or of disease in far distant lands, they had all died doing their duty. The town was proud of them one and all, officers, non-commissioned officers and men. They were worthy of the greatest gratitude and deepest homage. Mrs Buchanan concluded by declaring, 'To the undying memory of Yeovil's patriotic dead, I unveil this memorial.' She released a ribbon and the Union Jack fell away to reveal the large painting, thirteen feet tall by eight feet wide, which the *Western Gazette* described as:

> Depicting an angel, the Heavenly Messenger, laying a laurel wreath on a Latin cross upon which would be painted the names of those Yeovilians who died in the service of their country, and at the foot of the cross was laid a garland of red roses enclosing the Borough Arms.

The artist was Mr J. T. Randolph who was living in Yeovil at the time.

The Reverend W. G. Butt proposed the vote of thanks to Mrs Buchanan, to whom he said the town owed a deep gratitude for her many generous services. Mr J. Matthews, seconding, said that remembering his own pain (the name of one of his sons would be inscribed on the painting) everyone must thank her for her courage in coming here today. Mrs Buchanan had given them a great example in these terrible times and which had called for every bit of courage that was only characteristic of her. Mr Matthews would lose two more sons killed in the War.

The Vicar of Yeovil proposed a vote of thanks to the artist for his generous and ably performed gift, and paid high tribute to the work. Colonel Yates, Officer Commanding the Yeovil Volunteer Training Corps, seconded, and stated that the gift came at a most appropriate time when every man was wanted who could put his shoulder to the wheel. He hoped the picture now would help those who could not make up their minds to volunteer for service.

Mr Randolph, the artist, came forward to great applause, and thanked gathering for the way they had received his work.

The National Anthem was sung and the proceedings terminated. No one on that Saturday afternoon in February 1916 could foresee the terrible battles yet to come in which Yeovilians would lose their lives, the Somme, Passchendaele and the great offensives of 1918, and the effects the War would have on Great Britain, Europe and the World.

In July 1921 the War Memorial bearing the names of 226 Yeovilians who lost their lives in the First World War was unveiled in the Borough and to which has since been added the names of those who died in the Second, but the fate of the painting remains a mystery. Until I read about it in the 3 March 1916 edition of the *Western Gazette*, I had never heard of the painting. Was it destroyed in the Town Hall Fire of 1935, or was it quietly put away as the casualty lists grew and grew?

THE LOCAL MILITARY SERVICE TRIBUNAL

By the end of the first year of the First World War in the autumn of 1915, the Army's need to replace the high casualties being suffered on the Western Front and the increasing demands of the war effort, could not be met from voluntary sources. After much debate and opposition, the Military Service Act was passed and came into force at the beginning of February 1916, the first compulsory conscription law ever made in the Great Britain. Initially all single men and childless widowers aged eighteen to forty-one were registered for the call-up, and local Tribunals were formed to hear applications for exemption. During the remaining years of the War, the call-up would be extended to other categories and age groups as the Army's losses and manpower needs increased; more than 2.3 million men would be conscripted before the War was over.

The first application to be considered by the Yeovil Borough Tribunal in February 1916 was that of an un-named hairdresser who stated that he had invested all his capital in the business and his one assistant had already joined the Army. He was now working single-handed, and his widowed mother was dependent on him. His younger brother was in the Army, another was paralysed and could not work, and a third brother was working away in a munitions factory. Efforts to employ a new assistant had proved fruitless. The Tribunal granted a conditional exemption on grounds of hardship. The Tribunal granted temporary exemptions for one month to enable arrangements to be made for their replacements to a draper, gents' outfitter, a motor engineer's cashier and the son of a milk retailer; the application of a tailor was refused.

During the next three years the Borough Tribunal, under the Chairmanship of Councillor (later Alderman and Mayor) W. R. E. Mitchelmore, held seventy-two formal hearings and dealt with 2,686 applications. The applications came from a wide range of ages, occupations and situations, and I've selected a few of the cases to show what the members had to deal with. The Tribunal's proceedings were reported in the local press, and although in the beginning the names of applicants were withheld, within a few months names were given.

At the beginning of March 1916 the first two conscientious objectors presented their applications. One was a Sunday School Superintendent, who pleaded for absolute exemption as he was completely opposed to war, his mother was blind, his father had been operated upon three times for cataracts, and he had to look after his father's affairs. The Tribunal ignored the conscientious objection, but granted a conditional exemption on grounds of hardship. The second from a thirty-year-old glove cutter was refused as the Tribunal considered his objection was on political and not religious grounds.

At the hearing on 15 March 1917, Frederick Taylor, married, proprietor of a drapery, dressmaking and undertakers business and classed as Bi (work not of national importance) requested that he should not be given exemption on condition that he joined the Voluntary Aid Detachment of the British Red Cross or the Volunteer Training Corps, because the whole of his time was devoted to the work of the Boys' Brigade of which he was Captain of the Yeovil Company. The application was supported by the

Within a month of being refused deferment, Bert Jennings (3rd row second from left) and Reg Sweet (back row 3rd from left) were in training on Salisbury Plain.

Wessex Council of the Boys' Brigade who emphasised the importance of his work. Temporary exemption was granted to the 1 June next and no further appeal without leave. The application of a twenty-year-old glover, Frederick Glover, of Hillview, on grounds that he had been suffering from bronchial catarrh for six months was dismissed. The twelve other applications heard by the Tribunal included a commercial traveller, motor and agricultural engineer, groom/gardener, plumber, foreman mechanic and a head warehouseman, all of whom were given conditional exemptions to 1 August next.

On 26 April 1917, some twenty applications were heard including an accountant, foreman coach body builder, foreman printer, ironmonger, estate agent and auctioneer, master tailor, solicitor's clerk, who was also secretary of the Town Volunteer Fire Brigade, and a discharged soldier; the applicants were married and single with ages ranging from twenty to forty-one years.

I found the meeting of 13 September 1917 of special interest. Mr R. L. Hiscott, Clerk to the Tribunal, reported that he had received a recommendation from the military representatives regarding all the cases which would come before them this afternoon. Of the ninety-nine cases applied for, ninety-six should be given temporary exemption until 1 February 1918, E. Robbins aged thirty-nine, a manufacturer, an unconditional exemption. However those of R. W. Sweet, eighteen, single (Messrs Thring & Luffman), and B. Jennings, eighteen, single (Messrs Atherton & Clothier) should be dismissed as it was not in the national interest that they should be retained in civilian employment. The two young men had just completed their gloving apprenticeships. The Tribunal adopted the recommendation in full. The R. W. Sweet was my father Reg, and within one month both he and Bert Jennings had joined the Wiltshire Regiment. They were sent to France at the beginning of April 1918, but sadly Bert was killed two months later, and my father was badly wounded at the end of October a few weeks before the fighting ceased. It appeared that the reason for the ninety-six exemptions was that all the men were glovers and there were large Government contracts to be completed by the end of December 1917.

The last meeting of the Borough Tribunal was held on 31 October 1918 following the Local Government Board's decision to amalgamate the Borough and Rural District Tribunals. At this meeting the *Western Gazette* reported the following cases were heard:

> Alfred E. Stevens (41), married, Pen Park-road, cardboard box manufacturer, applied on several grounds, including that of certified occupation and that he was the directing head of a large business. The application was objected to. The Chairman stated that they understood that the business was entirely dependent on Mr Steven's control. Mr Kent Francis said that therefore he had the right to claim exemption on that ground. Temporary exemption to May 1st, to join the VAD.
>
> OTHER CASES. Henry R. S. Templeman (43), 25 Queen Street, miller (Bradford & Sons) Feb. 1st. William John Hewlett (41), 6 Rustywell, cartage contractor &c., May 1st. Alexander Buchanan (50), widower, North Lane, draper, February 1st and excused Volunteer condition. John Bonning (25), 20 Brunswick-street, painter &c, (Mr E. Minson), May 1st, to join the VAD. Harold Walter Larcombe (18), 64 St. Michael's Avenue, tailor's apprentice, adjourned for re-examination.

Eleven days later the guns fell silent and the War was over; the Tribunals were disbanded within a few months.

JULY

When Yeovilians read their *Western Gazettes* on Friday 7 July 1916 they would have been cheered to read of sweeping British successes, brilliant trench raids, fierce onslaughts, dauntless bravery, and the surrender of thousands of German troops. However, during the weeks and months to come, it would become apparent that the great battle which had begun and which would go down in history as the Battle of the Somme, was far from the brilliant sweeping successes being read about in Yeovil on that Friday in the first week of July.

Far from the battlefield, the Yeovil High School for Girls held its annual sports on Wednesday the 5th in the school grounds in The Park, and it was reported that there was some excellent running and jumping. The competition between the school forms

Yeovil High School for Girls.

The girls of Yeovil High School held their annual sports day on 5 July.

was described as 'spirited' and ended in a victory for Form V. However, no prizes were awarded as the competitors voted for all the money collected for the sports to be given to the fund for English Prisoners of War in Germany.

On the 4 July, an American Sale drew a large and enthusiastic crowd to the grounds of Swallowcliffe in Kingston, the home of Mr F. Whitmarsh Mayo, to raise funds for the Swallowcliffe Patriotic Working Party. The *Western Gazette* reported that 'The stalls were laden with fruit, cakes and miscellaneous articles and the sale was a great success.' Tea was served on the tennis lawn.

The Yeovil Patriotic Fête Committee met in the Municipal Offices on Wednesday evening, 5 July, to discuss holding the event at Newton Park during the coming August in aid of the Yeovil Hospital and the Yeovil Red Cross Hospital. A provisional programme was agreed to include athletic sports for old and young, swimming races and diving in the River Yeo, pony jumping and donkey racing, platform entertainments, side shows and 'varieties of various descriptions.' The Committee decided that both fields would be used on each side of the river.

The scholars of the Baptist Sunday School had their annual treat on 5 July, and St John's Church Sunday Schools held theirs the following day in a malthouse near the Clarence Street Brewery.

The Revd A. J. Waldron gave a lecture at the Albany Ward Palace Theatre in the Triangle, on 'What I Saw in France and Serbia' illustrated by 150 slides taken on the French and Serbian battlefields.

At the Nautilus Works in Reckleford (now the bus garage) Mr Ben Jacobs was presented with an Illuminated Address and a £100 War Loan Bond by the Directors of Petters Ltd, in recognition of his twenty-one-years service with the company, and for 'the valuable services rendered by him in connection with the design of the first Petter oil engine in 1895.'

The orders for the Volunteer Training Corps published in the *Western Gazette* for the week ending 8 July were:

> Sunday – Fall in at the Territorial Hall at 12 noon and march to Sherborne to take part in a military parade. Men have the option of attending an evening concert on returning to Yeovil after tea. Cyclists can take their machines and will march at the head of the column to Sherborne.
>
> Monday – Machine gun section at 8 pm.
>
> Tuesday – Parade in uniform. Field operations. 7.45 pm sharp.
>
> Wednesday – Recruits drill at 8 pm.

The Tuesday field operations involved the Volunteer Training Corps and the Men's Voluntary Aid Detachment in a combined scheme in Barwick Park. The *Western Gazette* reported that

> The V.A.D. and the V.T.C. met at the Town hall and marched up Hendford Hill to the Park. Here the Volunteers carried out an attack, and their supposed casualties were promptly dealt with and conveyed to a temporary dressing-station by the stretcher squads of the V.A.D. After the operations Col. Trask congratulated the Volunteers on the way they had occupied such a wide front with a small number of men and reserves, and the V.A.D. on their efficient bandaging and general work. The two detachments formed up and returned to their respective headquarters.

Meanwhile, across the English Channel in the real war and along with tens of thousands of their fellow countrymen, Yeovilians were fighting and dying in the trenches of the Western Front. At 7.30 on the morning of Saturday 1 July 1916, under a clear blue sky, some 750,000 British and French soldiers climbed out of their trenches and attacked the German positions on the Somme. By the end of that summer day, the British army had suffered over 58,000 casualties, a third of them killed, and more casualties than on any other day in its history.

Amongst the dead and missing were Yeovilians Private Albert Helyar from 25 Great Western Terrace, and Private Bertie Chant from 45 Queen Street, and Corporal Reginald Pennell, late of 154 Park Street, would die on 2 July from wounds received on the 1st. All three young men were serving in the First Battalion of the Somerset Light Infantry. The First and Eighth Battalions of the Somersets had gone over the top on 1 July and between them lost 44 officers and 863 other ranks killed, wounded or missing on that first day of the Somme.

Albert Helyar is remembered on the great Thiepval Memorial to the Missing, together with the names of 73,367 men who died on the Somme and who have no known graves. Bertie Chant lies in Sucrerie Military Cemetery, Colin Camps, Somme, and Reginald Pennell in the Couin British Cemetery, Pas de Calais.

On Sunday evening 9 July, the first wounded from the Battle of the Somme arrived at the Red Cross Hospital and the *Western Gazette* reported that 'A large crowd witnessed the unloading of the stretchers and commented on the careful handling of the wounded men by the V.A.D.'

The Battle of the Somme would continue for another four months until November 1916. The British would suffer over 420,000 casualties, the French almost 200,000 and the Germans some 500,000.

NOVEMBER

Two November weddings in 1916 caught the eye of the Editor of the *Western Gazette*:

Friday 17 November
WAR HERO'S MARRIAGE
The wedding took place on Saturday at St John's Church of Mr. J. Jackson, of 11 Westville, and late of Walthamstow, to Mrs. L. A. Barrett, late of Sherborne, whose husband was killed in Gallipoli on August 21st 1915. Both bride and bridegroom are connected with the local corps of the Salvation Army, the former being for some time a Young People's "Sergeant-Major" in the Sherborne corps. Mr. J. Jackson was called up as a reservist at the commencement of hostilities, and was drafted with his regiment, the Essex, to Gallipoli, where he was mentioned three times in despatches for good all-round work, sniping and bringing in two wounded men. He was wounded on August 16th 1915, and was awarded the Distinguished Conduct Medal and the French honour – the Croix de Guerre. Mr. Jackson still has a bullet in his head.

Friday 1 December
MARRIAGE OF A VETERAN COUPLE
An interesting presentation took place on Friday at Messrs. Hawkins, Jesty & Ricketts' dressing yard, when Mr. John Mooney, of 92 Eastland Road, an old age pensioner, was the recipient of an arm-chair and a picture subscribed by his fellow employees, in recognition of his impending marriage to Mrs. Tutton, of 58 Westville. The marriage took place on Sunday at the South Street Primitive Methodist Chapel, the Rev. Mr. Sunderland performing the ceremony. The couple were attended by Mr. and Mrs. E. W. Bush, and the bridegroom's two grandchildren Gwennie and Elsie Parfitt. The bride, who is 64 years of age and the bridegroom 73, were the recipients of a number of hearty congratulations.

Other celebrations of a more public nature included a concert in St Michael's Hall on behalf of the *Daily Telegraph* Shilling Fund for providing Christmas puddings for the troops on the Western Front. The Hall was packed to capacity, and the audience enjoyed 'songs, violin solos, whistling solos, vocal duets, and a piano forte selection of popular melodies. duets and solos. The contributors to the programme were Misses Olive Tucker, Elsie Davis, Hilda Grant, Ada Tucker and Rose Parsons, and Messrs. E. J. Sutton, R. Seward, R. Tucker and E. Easthouse.'

Some 200 Soldiers and Sailors' wives and mothers were entertained to tea in the Salvation Army Temple at the junction of Newton Road and Middle Street, on 6 November. There were two sittings followed by a concert of piano and vocal solos, and a selection of musical numbers by the Young People's Band.

The Town Hall was the venue for a jumble sale on the 7th organized by Mrs. Rose Buchanan, the widow of the late mayor, in aid of the purchase of X-ray equipment for the Red Cross Military Hospital and the Prisoners of War Fund. All the items were sold raising £20 3s 6d for the X-ray equipment and £5 for the POWs.

On the municipal 'front', Alderman Damon, who had stepped in to take up the office of Mayor following the sudden death of Councillor Norman Buchanan in January, was unanimously relected Mayor at the Borough Council's annual meeting on 8 November.

In its report to the Council, the Gas Committee (the Council ran the town gas works), referred to a reduction in demand of nearly ten percent. Supplies of coal were coming through, and the works were operating satisfactorily. However some difficulties were being experienced because of labour shortages. Twenty-six men had joined the Army, three had lost their lives and a similar number wounded, including the assistant manager, Mr Fenwick, who had now returned to duty following his discharge as medically unfit. The Committee chairman stated that all the present employees were working under considerable difficulties and went on to say that 'Had it not been for their devotion and willingness to do any job asked of them, the town would have been without gas on more than one occasion.'

The weather in late October and early November 1916 was awful; in the first week of November over four inches of rain were recorded at the town gas works at the bottom of Middle Street. Gales with torrential rain tore across the West Country and beginning on Saturday evening, 3 November, and continuing all day Sunday, the wind blew and rain poured down continuously. The River Yeo broke its banks flooding the surrounding fields and the normally placid Hendford Brook had been turned into a raging torrent. No property was flooded but there was one tragedy.

Rivers and streams in flood seem to be a magnet for boys (and grown ups), but the attraction would sadly be fatal for eight-year-old Leonard Little of 9 Felix Place. Leonard and his friends were enjoying their half-term holiday from Huish Boys School and on the Friday concerned they had assembled to watch the Brook as it roared in the cutting between Horsey Lane and Bradford's Yard and through the bridge under Hendford Hill. Obviously wishing to show off his daring, Leonard squeezed through the railing fence on the Horsey Lane side and began to walk along the ledge at the top of the culvert shouting to his friends to watch him as he was not holding on. There was a sudden strong gust of wind, Leonard stumbled, over balanced, and fell into the torrent. The poor lad did not stand a chance, and within moments he disappeared into the tunnel under Hendford Hill and was not seen again.

Leonard Little's body was found under the bank of gardens at the rear of Brunswick Street.

Search parties scouring the banks of the Hendford Brook were handicapped by the force and the height of the water and it was not until the level fell on the following day that his body was found under the bank of gardens at the rear of Brunswick Street.

The inquest returned a verdict that Leonard Little was accidently drowned and added a rider that a more substantial fence should be provided with immediate effect. The jury donated their fees to the X-ray equipment fund.

The staff of the Fitting Shop of Westland Aircraft in 1917.

1917

MARCH

In Mesopotamia (now Iraq), after a series of successful battles, the British Army captured Baghdad from the Turks, but on the Western Front, success against the German Army could almost be counted in yards rather than miles.

Back in Yeovil there was both sadness and hope in the news coming from the various theatres of operation. Tragedy struck the Hardy household when Mr and Mrs Hardy of Victoria Road received the news that their nineteen-year-old son, Fred, a sapper in the Royal Engineers, had died of wounds, the second son they had lost in the war. Mr and Mrs Ellis of 51 Wellington Street were doubtless very relieved to hear that their twenty-five-year-old son, Victor, previously reported missing, was a prisoner of war in Germany.

The Rogers brothers of Crofton Avenue, William and Charlie, were both in hospital, Royal Marine William, with a broken arm from an accident on board his ship, and Charlie with a shrapnel wound in his left thigh received on the Western Front. Private Sinnick, of the South Wales Borderers, whose wife lived in Church Terrace, was reported seriously wounded in Mesopotamia, shortly after recovering from a bout of dysentery.

Lieutenant W. E. Somervell, of the Royal Flying Corps, who had been shot down and was a prisoner of war, wrote to friends;

I am quite well now. We have been having very frosty weather just lately and much skating, but I wish I was back again at Petters. Shall hope to see you soon. What! Our camp is at Krieg gefangenenlager, Gutersloh, Germany (Offizier). Don't fall over the address.

A former *Western Gazette* printer, Private S. Hallett, serving with the Somerset Light Infantry, was in a Liverpool hospital suffering from trench foot, as were twelve of the fourteen stretcher cases brought straight from the Front to the Red Cross Military Hospital in the Newnam Memorial Hall.

Some thirty wounded soldiers were entertained at the Masonic Hall by the Holy Trinity Girls' Friendly Society, 'Numerous games were provided and a musical programme carried out.'

The teachers and youngsters of the Pen Mill Congregational Sunday School laid on a tea and amusements for a party of wounded soldiers and which the men were said to have greatly appreciated.

At Mr Albany Ward's Picture Palace in the Triangle, the official War Office Film of the Battle of the Ancre, was being shown to full houses and the *Western Gazette* wrote that

> It is undoubtedly the best war picture yet taken, and graphically shows trench life, the advance of the 'tanks', some of the great British guns, and the awe-inspiring effect they produce at night. The cheery optimism of our troops when returning from the trenches laden with 'captures from Fritz' and the devotion and care given to our wounded, are features in a series of wonderful pictures.

The film might not have been so popular if the bodies of the dead and mutilated British soldiers had been shown, which of course they weren't!

Mr Sam Willie and a friend, had a day's fishing in the River Yeo at Pen Mill, and landed some 60 lbs of coarse fish which were sent to London for sale. The proceeds of £2 13s 7d were given to the organisers of the Red Cross Military Hospital.

A civilian casualty was Mr Foote, of Colmer Road, who was cycling from West Coker to Yeovil, when his front wheel was caught in a rut in the road, and he was thrown over the handlebars. The cyclist sustained a severely cut leg and sprained ankle, which sent him to bed for a few days to recover.

There were increasing shortages of foodstuffs, caused in part by the great losses of merchant ships sunk by German U-boats, and under Government directions as much land as possible was being brought into cultivation. At the beginning of March meeting, the Borough Council was concerned at a growing potato shortage and rocketing prices because growers appeared to be holding stocks off the markets. The councillors were alarmed to hear that on the previous Saturday, there had been no potatoes to be bought in Yeovil. It was resolved to write to the National Food Controller and suggest that the time had come for all potato stocks in England to be commandeered. The Council were informed that a further 140 allotment plots had been allocated including some on Mr Willie's land at the top of Hendford Hill and a crop of swedes grown on spare Council land at the Pen Mill Sewage Works had been sold for £7. The shortage of agricultural workers was also causing concern, and the Army was being used to help with the problem. Enemy prisoners of war were also being brought in, but a plan to use forty Germans in the Yeovil area was put on hold because of the difficulty in providing guards.

There was alarm at the Cattle Market on 7 March when a large bull calf bounded out of the wagon as it was being unloaded into a pen. Despite breaking a leg the bull calf charged about the yard, knocking over a bystander before the terrified beast was shot dead.

From these seats in Mr Albany Ward's Picture Palace, the audience watched 'The best war picture yet taken'.

The *Western Gazette's* edition of 9 March included the following letter to the Editor from Colonel W. M. Marsh, of Old Sarum House in Princes Street:

> Might I suggest that it would be in accordance with the wishes of many inhabitants, if a memorial were erected in the town to the memory of all the brave Yeovil men who have given their lives in the service of our country in this war?
>
> It has been suggested that it should take the form of a large stone cross, with all the names inscribed on it, and that it should stand in some open space, such as the Parish Churchyard, which is now under the care of the Town Council.

Colonel Marsh had lost his elder son, Captain Edward Marsh of the Indian Army. He had drowned when the liner *Persia* was torpedoed by the German U-boat *U-38*, and sank in the Mediterranean, on 30 December 1915. Captain Marsh had seen active service on the Western Front and at Gallipoli where he had been wounded, and was travelling on the ill-fated ship to rejoin his regiment in India following a short stay with his parents in Yeovil.

FLAX

Flax is a very versatile plant, the fibres from its stem are used to produce linen fabrics, ropes and twine, and its seeds are used in the manufacture of linseed oil.

For several hundred years the crop was grown extensively in and around Yeovil, but with stiff competition from Northern Ireland and the continent, and from Belgium in particular, the local industry had contracted to a small acreage at the beginning of the last century.

Two booklets *Flax and Hemp: A Local History* written by the late Mr Leslie Brooke and published by the Museum of South Somerset in 1993, and *Early Flax Growing: The Flax Industry of the Cokers* by Mr Robert G. Allwood, are excellent histories and descriptions of the industry in this area.

In 1912, however, the British Flax & Hemp Growers' Society with Government support, sought to re-introduce the industry in South Somerset. Fifty acres were sown in Preston Plucknett at Abbey Farm in 1912, fifty more in 1913 and another fifty in 1914. With the outbreak of War there was a huge demand for flax products for military purposes, one being the use of linen fabric to cover airframes in the rapidly expanding aircraft industry. The loss of supplies from Belgium and the continent could only be met by increasing the acreage in Great Britain.

It was said that remarkably good fibre was produced in South Somerset, and some 420 acres had been planted by the 1917 season with flax processing factories at Abbey Farm and Bunford and depots at South Petherton and Lopen. Traditionally, flax was

Hard-working lady 'flax-pullers' take a well-earned break.

harvested by hand, flax pulling, and because the introduction of a mechanical harvester in 1916 had not been a success, harvesting returned to the old and tried flax pulling. However, labour was in short supply and in July 1917, 105 soldiers from a home defence battalion of the Yorkshire Regiment were drafted in to help with the harvest, together with 100 women and girls of the Womens' National Land Service Corps. The soldiers were billeted in Preston Plucknett and several surrounding villages and the ladies lodged in Barwick House.

The pulled flax, after de-seeding and soaking to release the fibres, was brought to the factories at Abbey Farm and Bunford for final treatment. This entailed 'scutching' by machine which separated the flax from the weedy stalk of the plant and left the fibres ready for spinning and weaving.

One problem of growing flax close to Yeovil was damage caused by people going into the fields to pick wild flowers. In July 1917, several young girls were brought before the town magistrates charged with damaging a crop at Aldon Farm in their search for corn flowers. The Chairman of the Bench stated that the cases had not been brought to inflict heavy fines but to draw attention to the damage being caused to this important crop. The cases were proven and the girls fined one shilling each.

In July and August 1918, Barwick House and grounds was the home of 600 young women brought in for the harvest flax pull. They came from far and wide, Miss Rentoul and Miss Baxter brought ten 'gangs' from Fife in Scotland, others came from English universities and colleges and there was a large contingent of the Women's Land Army. Some came for three weeks others for six and all could work up to nine hours a day pulling the flax plants on farms around the district.

On 9 August, the *Western Gazette* published a letter from one of the Scots girls:

> Miss Rintoul had charge of the arrangements and did every thing in her power for their comfort in camp, while with Miss Baxter as the leader in the field the girls felt quite prepared for the Fife harvest. The camp life was most enjoyable and all the gangs regret that their sojourn in Yeovil was so soon terminated. They much appreciated the untiring efforts of the Commandant, Miss Bennet and her staff who worked most conscientiously and harmoniously. Despite the fact that the weather was not the most favourable, they nevertheless proved most advantageous to the training, as every aspect of flax harvest was brought into operation. Most of the workers speak in very high terms of the kindness they received at the hands of the Somerset people.

On 27 August P. J., one of the flax pullers, sent a postcard of Barwick House to Mrs Judd at Ardleigh, Essex:

> Today has come on wet so since lunch at 12.30, we have been lying in the straw in a barn, very comfy, we have also slept. Being now refreshed by tea and having finished my book, a deadly dull one I have borrowed a fountain pen and am writing this. There is still an hour to wait for the lorry and we have been passing the time tickling each other with straws as we try to go to sleep. How do you like the look of B. House? The lake is somewhat filled in now but is to be drained again when the new occupants

come. The last went bankrupt. Next week the camp will close as nearly all the girls will have gone. There are about a 100 left now. B. House is our YWCA and hospital etc. You know we are working at Montacute where L. Curzon's house is. It is lovely.

Despite the local flax providing good quality fibre, the fall in demand following the end of the War and the recession of the 1920s, resulted in the run down of the industry and the works at Abbey Farm and Bunford closed.

A 'WELL-KNOWN AVIATOR'

On 17 August 1917, the *Western Gazette* ran the following story:

> Captain True, a well-known aviator, who for several months resided in Yeovil, and tested many of the machines manufactured at Westland, has fallen in with adventures since he left Yeovil. A Central News telegram, published on Monday says: Captain Ronald True, of the Royal British Flying Corps. Now an instructor for the Eastern Aeroplane Company, of Brooklyn, has had a remarkable escape from death.
>
> He was flying with Mr William Reed, a student in the school at the Sheepshead Bay Speedway, when his motor stopped and the machine crashed down from a height of a hundred feet. Both planes were smashed and the whole machine practically demolished.
>
> Men from the military training camp established at the Speedway rushed to expecting to find both men dead. Instead they found Captain True and Mr Reed bruised and bleeding but conscious. Captain True thanked the men for their prompt assistance and then asked if anyone had found his 'charmed pilot cap,' an involuntary gift from one of the German aviators brought to earth by the Captain at the Front, and also enquired for his mascot.
>
> Both were found in the wreckage, and the two men were subsequently taken to hospital, where it was found that Mr Reed's knees were painfully injured.
>
> The Yankee correspondent continues: 'Captain True brought down fourteen German aeroplanes, and was wounded seven times before he came to America to instruct aviators. In his last encounter he was shot through the hip and maimed for life.
>
> He recently married a Mrs Earle of Wilmington, Delaware, and according to the papers, he proposed when they were in an aeroplane 5,000 feet in the air.

What a story and what a man! Sadly Captain True did not live up to his name. Ronald True grew up in comfortable circumstances but his petty thieving, lying and cheating resulted in his being sent abroad in the hope this would improve his behaviour. It didn't, and he was sacked from a number of jobs, but in 1915 he returned to England and somehow obtained a commission in the Royal Flying Corps. Following a flying accident during training at Farnborough he was injured and invalided out of the service; he saw no flying action over the Western Front, downed no German

Yeovil from the Air. 90621

One of Captain Ronald True's exploits was flying low over the town at roof-top height.

aircraft and was not wounded seven times. However, in 1917 he came to Yeovil testing Westland aircraft for several months, and was considered to be a dare devil pilot. During this time, one of his exploits was a flight down Middle Street at roof-top height, but following a series of minor crashes, Ronald True left the company and departed for the United States.

In May 1922, following a trial which gripped the public's imagination, Ronald True was found guilty at the Old Bailey of murdering a 'better class prostitute' Gertrude Yates, alias Olive Young, and despite strong pleas that he was insane, was sentenced to death. However, Ronald True was reprieved, the sentence commuted to life imprisonment, and he was committed to Broadmoor where he died in 1951.

SEPTEMBER

In the first week of September 1917, the First World War was entering its third year. Just across the English Channel in Flanders, the Third Battle of Ypres (which would come down to us as the Battle of Passchendaele) was entering its third terrible month, and when the campaign ground to a halt in the following November, the British Expeditionary Force had lost over 300,000 men dead, wounded or captured.

On 7 September, it was reported in the columns of *Western Gazette*, that Private Sutton of Yeovil had been killed in action, Privates Sibley and A'Court also of Yeovil, were wounded, Private Pippard of Preston Plucknett was missing, and Lieutenant Baker

Convalescent wounded soldiers enjoying a trip out.

of West Coker was dead. Private Wiscombe from East Coker, was reported gassed, Mrs Purchase of Hardington Mandeville heard that her husband had fallen in action, and Privates Penny and Weeks of Ilchester were wounded. On the credit side, if there was one, the *Gazette* reported that Sergeant H. J. Bagwell of Yeovil, who had served nearly two years on the Western Front, had been awarded the Military Medal for bravery in the field.

Conscription was now in full swing, and the Local Tribunal set up to deal with applications for exemption, deferral, etc., from military service, met and heard applications from four men residing in the Yeovil rural district. One was from a single gardener, chauffeur and motor mechanic of Stoke-sub-Hamdon, who had already been discharged from the Army as medically unfit. However, because the Army needed mechanics, exemption from further service was only granted for a month. The case of a married innkeeper and farmer from Ash was referred to the County War Agricultural Committee, as were those of two agricultural workers.

The wounded soldiers under treatment at the Red Cross Hospital in the Newnam Memorial Hall on South Street were entertained by the Bowling Club to afternoon tea provided by members' wives at the green in Huish.

One soldier, who had probably seen too much war, was found in a railway truck at Pen Mill Station, arrested and brought before the Town magistrates charged with being an absentee from the Wiltshire Regiment's camp at Littlemore, Upwey, Weymouth. The soldier, who came from Leicester, admitted to having no pass and being an absentee, and was remanded to await an escort back to his unit. The *Western Gazette's* court reporter, noted that the soldier wore a wound stripe and had been in the Army since

1914; the veteran's fate remains unknown.

Over £100 was raised for the National Egg Collection for Wounded Soldiers and Sailors, from street collections, the sale of lavender bags, and a whist drive and dance in the Town Hall.

In the late summer of 1917, German submarine attacks on our ocean lifeline were becoming very serious, and early in September, a Borough Food Control Committee was established, and a Food Control Office opened in South Street. The *Western Gazette* reported that

> With regard to meat prices, it is understood that there was little alteration in the local market on Monday, despite the orders fixing retail prices, but butchers, who have formed an Association, have drawn up a scale of prices which are now being displayed in the shops and have been submitted to the Food Control Committee. With regard to the Sugar Control Scheme, the Committee have not yet received posters or forms of application to register, but all the facts and instructions will be issue to the public immediately they are received.

The following week, however, the forms for the Sugar Control Scheme were received, and one was sent to all householders in the town for them to register for a sugar ration. The forms had to be returned to the Food Control Office by the 5 October, and those householders who had not received the forms were advised to apply to the Post Office. Shopkeepers wishing to retail sugar had to apply before 15 September and caterers before the 22nd.

Looking through the columns of the *Western Gazette* of 7 September 1917, there seems little to cheer the reader, and the following report under the headline 'THREE MORE YEARS OF WAR' could be even more depressing.

> Mr Lord, an American delegate told the Trades Union Congress at Blackpool on Thursday, that American workers were making plans on the assumption that it would take three years to win the war.

Mercifully, the Americans' plans would not be necessary as the War ended fourteen months later on 11 November 1918.

THE FIRST WESTLAND CRASH – SEPTEMBER 1917

At about half-past ten on Monday morning, 3 September 1917, Flight Sub-Lieutenant John Emyr Thomas of the Royal Naval Air Service, an Air Department ferry pilot, took off in his Avro 504E two-seat bi-plane from Westland's airfield *en route* for the Royal Naval Air Station Hendon. Accompanying the Flight Sub-Lieutenant in the observer's seat behind him was Mr Robert Norton, Westland's commercial director, on his way to a meeting with Air Board in London.

The take off was normal, but at about 300 feet, the aircraft banked sharply to the left and nose-dived into a field near the bridge over the Yeovil to Taunton railway line at Bunford. Rescuers from the factory arrived at the crash within minutes and found Mr Norton pinned under the aircraft's fuel tank, still alive but badly injured. Mercifully the plane had not caught fire, the injured man was carefully extracted from the wreckage and rushed to Yeovil Hospital in the Red Cross ambulance which had now arrived on the scene. Sadly the young Naval pilot was found to have died in the crash.

The inquest into the death of twenty-three-year-old, Flight Sub-Lieutenant J. E. Thomas before Mr E. Q. Louch, the coroner and his jury, was held on 5 September. The first witness was Mr Percy Warren, the Westland assistant manager, who stated that the Avro bi-plane had flown down to the factory from Hendon, on the Monday previous to the accident. The officer had taken a new plane back, and left instructions for the Avro to be returned by another pilot. Flight Sub-Lieutenant Thomas had arrived at the works early on Monday morning for this flight, and the witness stated that he had accompanied the officer and Mr Norton to the aircraft. There had been some trouble starting the engine, but it was running well when the Avro taxied out and took off. Mr Warren stated that the aircraft had flown some 600 yards and risen to a height of about 300 feet when it banked to the left and got into a vertical spin until about 100 feet off the ground when it took a nose-dive. With other employees he had rushed to the scene of the crash and found the aircraft a total wreck. Mr Warren went on to say that at no time had the flight sub-lieutenant expressed any doubts about the condition of the aircraft prior to take off.

Squadron Commander Evill, DSC, Royal Naval Air Service, representing the Air Board, testified that the deceased officer was fully qualified to fly the Avro 504E, and was in fact flying an aircraft easier to handle than those he was used to. The Squadron Commander believed that the pilot had been over-confident with the machine and had made an error, which if he had been flying higher, he might have corrected. Flight Sub-Lieutenant Thomas had been used to more powerful aircraft, and had been too low when he banked. The witness went on to say that Mr Norton, the passenger, who was too ill to attend to give evidence, had told him that the engine was running perfectly at the time, and thought the aircraft had been banked too steeply.

John Hardie, an engine mechanic employed by the Royal Aircraft Factory at Westland, took the stand, and testified that when the engine had failed to start, a short circuit had been found and rectified, but afterwards it had run smoothly. On the morning concerned, Flight Sub-Lieutenant Thomas had asked if anyone knew anything about the engine because he had flown in similar machines but had no experience of this one. Mr Hardie stated that,

> Lieutenant Thomas had no doubt flown this type of machine, but with a different engine, one of lower power. Deceased got out two fire extinguishers from the hangar, an unusual thing for a pilot to do, he having heard no doubt, that the type of engine sometimes caught fire. He also asked for the seat to be packed so that his feet could more easily reach the rudder-bar, and some sacks were brought, which brought his feet forward. When he got off the engine was running well. He told the witness that he did not like the type of engine. Witness had seen a good many of this type of engine in

An AVRO 504 similar to the one in which Flight Sub-Lieutenant Thomas died on take-off.

that particular type of machine. When it left the ground the machine seemed all right, and in witness's opinion, deceased 'pushed up the nose' of the machine too much in climbing. He had seen the machine arrive at the works and the engine had been running well. It was of the rotary type.

John Hardie was the last witness, and in his summing up, the coroner stated that in flying an aeroplane, a good deal must be left to the skill of the pilot upon whom everything depended.

When a man was in the air at a considerable altitude, it was impossible to tell what he was doing, or whether he came to grief through an error of judgment or a temporary stoppage of the engine, or defect in the engine or machine. There was the opinion of the commander that the sub-lieutenant was flying in over-confidence, and any evolution he could have made in a more powerful machine might not have come off in the one he was flying. They were assured that the machine ascended well. What caused the accident was a matter of speculation, but the machine came into a position which brought about a nose dive, and crashed to earth, causing injuries to the sub-lieutenant which cause his immediate death.

The jury found a verdict of 'accidental death, sustained whilst flying a Service bi-plane, which fell, the accident being probably due to over-confidence of the deceased in flying.' They also added that they were of the opinion that officers should not be called upon to fly machines with the engine of which they were not conversant.

The coroner stated that he would send the jury's opinion to the Air Board, and closed the inquest by expressing his sympathy to the relatives of the late officer who had lost his life in the execution of his duty just as much as a soldier or sailor of the King lost in direct action.

The body of Flight Sub-Lieutenant John Emyr Thomas was taken under the escort of the Yeovil Volunteers and two Royal Naval Air Service officers, from the Hospital to the Town Station on its last journey home to rest in the Rhewl Calvanistic Methodist Chapel Yard, near Ruthin in Denbighshire.

After twelve months recovering from his serious injuries, Mr Robert Norton returned to work.

FROM THE FILES

The Western Gazette 20 November 1914
Private Gazette Christmas Cards
The Western Gazette Co. Ltd. beg to intimate to their patrons that the sample books of their cards are now ready and may be viewed at the Printing Department, Sherborne-road, Yeovil, or they will be sent for customers' inspection on receipt of a postcard. These books contain some of the most beautiful and unique designs and are priced so as to meet the needs and purses of everyone. They range from 2s per dozen upwards. Persons wishing to send to their friends abroad should, take their selection at once so as to secure the pick of the books. Also see our Patriotic Greeting Cards selection suitable for sending to our soldiers and sailors.

The Western Gazette 26 March 1915
A Child's Mysterious Disappearance
A sensation was created in the town on Wednesday when it became known that the four-and-a-half-year-old son of Adjutant Kersey, the local officer of the Salvation Army, had mysteriously disappeared. From information obtained it appears that the child attended the Reckleford School in the morning as was his custom. He, however, did not arrive home for dinner, and was absent from school in the afternoon. Enquiries were made by the Adjutant and as he did not put in an appearance during the early part of the evening, information was given to the police, who at once took the matter in hand. Parties of SA and BP Boy Scouts, Boys' Brigade members, and a large number of townspeople were organized and a search of the district was made with the aid of hurricane and other lamps and this extended in some parts until the early part of yesterday (Thursday) morning but the child could not be traced.

Exhaustive enquiries were instituted in the morning and a more thorough search was made in the locality, several sections of the Army Service Corps helping in the work but their efforts proved futile. In the afternoon a large number of Territorials continued the search and an impression of the child was exhibited outside the Salvation Army Hall but no tidings of the missing lad could be obtained. The painful anxiety of the parents was relieved just after four o'clock on Thursday afternoon, when the news arrived of the discovery of the boy at Dorchester Railway-station at two o'clock on Wednesday afternoon. The boy arrived safely home between five and six o'clock on Thursday afternoon and all the little fellow could say about it was that 'he got into the train for a ride'. He was well taken care of during the time at Dorchester and appeared none the worse for the adventure, to the unspeakable joy of his distressed parents.

The Western Gazette 2 July 1915
Owner's Life Saved by His Dog
In the early hours of Thursday morning a fire broke out at 'Casula', Princes Street, the residence of Mr F. G. McDonnell, surgeon dentist, which had it not been for the intelligent act of Mr McDonnell's dog, an Airedale, might have had serious consequences. The fire broke at three o'clock in the dining room and apparently remained undiscovered by anyone except the dog who rushed upstairs and roused his master.

Mr McDonnell, who was in the house alone, his wife and daughter being at Sidmouth, was alarmed to find his room so full of smoke that he could not get down the stairs. He gave the alarm from the bedroom window, and his calls were heard by Miss G. Marsh in Old Sarum House opposite, and her father Colonel Marsh brought over a ladder by which Mr McDonnell escaped. When in the street he remembered that the dog was still in the house and he went back and after groping about in the thick smoke was able to find it and get it out.

Meanwhile, Mr Harry Watts was on the scene with his garden hose and the Fire Brigade was called, and were quickly on the scene. With their appliances they had no difficulty in subduing the outbreak, which, however, was sufficiently serious to practically destroy the whole contents of the dining room.

Seeing that the fire broke out at such a time and seemingly got a good hold, the dog in rousing his master probably saved his life and the destruction of much property.

The Western Gazette 3 March 1916
The Snowstorms
One of the heaviest snowfalls for many years has been experienced in the town and district during the weekend and the surrounding hills have quite an Arctic appearance. Although it has had the effect of checking the forward growth of plant life, and has been welcomed by gardeners, people using the public thoroughfares have found it very unpleasant. On Monday morning the snow was fast disappearing in the bright sunshine. There were several slips of snow from roof tops on Sunday, which made it dangerous for those using the pavement. One slip in particular was on the premises of Messrs. Oliver's, in Middle Street, where the globes of the large gaslights outside were completely smashed. Owing to the wires having been broken down, telephonic communication between Yeovil and Sherborne ceased. The motor mail which runs between Yeovil and Ilminster broke down at South Petherton on the return journey on Saturday morning and another car had to be dispatched to fetch the mails. Further heavy falls occurred during Monday and Tuesday nights.

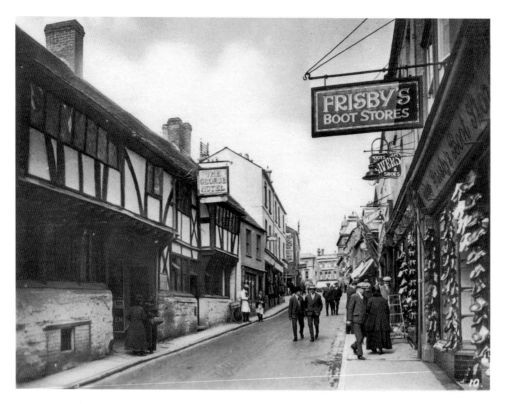

The gaslights outside Messrs Olivers' shop were smashed when snow slipped off the roof.

The Western Gazette 13 December 1918

A Dramatic Return

Private Edwin T. Hooper of the 2nd Devons, son of Mr and Mrs A. Hooper of Eastland-road, had a dramatic return home on Wednesday. It was only on the previous Friday, that his parents received information through the Red Cross that he had been reported to have died of wounds whilst a prisoner of war in Germany, and his unexpected arrival was a great shock to them. He was looking well despite hardships. He joined the Army in June 1917, and went to France in March 1918, and on 27 May was taken prisoner. For two months he was employed behind the German lines, and then taken inland to a glass factory. During the whole of his captivity Private Hooper received no correspondence. Before joining up he was employed as a cabinet-maker by Messrs. Raymond Brothers, in Manor Road.

1918

MAY

Arising from the effective German U-Boat campaign in the Western Approaches to Great Britain during the winter of 1917/18, and the continued sinking of large numbers of ships bringing supplies of food from the United Sates and Canada, the Government introduced rationing in February 1918. Ration books were issued to every family and retailers were strictly controlled. By May, rationing covered a wide range of basic foods from bacon to sweets. The Defence of the Realm Act, gave widespread powers to Government departments and local authorities to regulate many aspects of everyday life, including draconian powers to control supplies and commandeer land for food production. Local committees were established by councils to deal with the food controls, and the Yeovil Borough Food Committee at its meeting on 7 May discussed the co-ordination of road transport to give priority to the movement of food, the supply of potatoes to local bakers for bread making, the proposed new national scheme for food control, the reduction of sugar from ten pounds weight to six pounds per person for jam making, and the problems of butchers selling sausages with ration coupons. The Committee declined the request by a Pen Mill baker, accompanied by a petition, for support in his application for deferment from military service, and likewise a request from an inspector of national kitchens to establish a national kitchen in Yeovil was declined as the Committee felt there was no pressing need at present.

During its bid to help ease the food shortage, the Borough Council's Allotments Committee was able to report that there were now 1,550 fully occupied plots covering some 126 acres of ground, 40 of which were outside the Borough boundary. The Chairman, Councillor Higdon, believed that no other town in the West of England could show a better record and praise was due to all the men who worked so hard on the allotments.

Despite the gloom of four years of war and food rationing, the Whitsun Bank Holiday seems to have been much enjoyed. The weather was warm and sunny and despite crowded trains, large numbers of townsfolk went to the seaside. Many disappointed would-be travellers on the 8.45 train from Pen Mill to Weymouth were turned away. The 9.45 train from Town Station to Taunton was packed with families travelling the little way up the line to Montacute; they were all on their way for a day out on Ham Hill instead of the coast (imagine a train trip from Yeovil for Ham Hill!). It was commented that rarely had so many people visited Ham Hill on a bank holiday.

During the evening of 16 May, the pupils of Huish Girls' School (Tesco's garage now stands on the site) gave an 'excellent entertainment' in the Princes Street Assembly Rooms in aid of the Red Cross Military Hospital. The programme included two plays, one by the juniors 'The Duke of Christmas Daisies' and the senior girls presented 'The Court of King Cole'. There were songs, choruses and recitations. Mr M. W. Ring's orchestra provided the musical accompaniment and played concert selections. The *Western Gazette* reported that the 'youthful performances was good and the dresses, many of them quaint and humorous, were very effective'.

Mr Ring's orchestra had been engaged during the previous week's Thursday evening to play selections and accompaniments at an entertainment laid on at the Red Cross Military Hospital by the Men's Voluntary Aid Detachment. The patients, nursing staff, supporters and friends, enjoyed a whist drive, refreshments with tobacco and cigars, and musical numbers both vocal and instrumental.

There was 'entertainment' of sorts to some onlookers, when a cow being driven to market through High Street on 10 May, decided to 'investigate' the interior of Messrs Gamis's shop. Pushing through the door into the shop full of customers, the cow took fright and as it tried to escape smashed one of the plate glass windows. The *Western Gazette* reported that 'little damage was done, though some excitement was caused amongst the customers and assistants'.

A week later, a steer being driven to Messrs Parkers butchers' slaughterhouse at Silver Street, suddenly bolted as it passed the Three Choughs Hotel and galloped into High Street and through the Borough, knocking over a Mrs Garrett of St Michael's Avenue, leaving her shaken but uninjured. The steer was finally lassoed in Middle Street and taken to its fate.

Meanwhile in France and Belgium, as well as other zones of conflict, humans were slaughtering each other on an industrial scale. Twenty-six-year-old Private Henry Whittaker of the Machine Gun Corps, finally succumbed to his wounds in the Red Cross Military Hospital, having been brought to Yeovil from the Western Front on 16 April. His coffin draped with a Union flag, was driven to Town Station at the start of the soldier's final journey home to Liverpool.

Across in France, on 30 May, the 2nd Battalion of the Wiltshire Regiment was dug in by the village of Chambrecy, near Reims, awaiting a German attack. This came during the early morning, but after a stout resistance the Wiltshires were ordered to withdraw to avoid being outflanked. However, the battalion counter attacked the next day and captured some high ground north west of Chambrecy, but in the process suffered high casualties in dead and wounded. Yeovilian, Lance-Corporal Bert Jennings was killed in the attack, and now lies in Chambrecy Military Cemetery.

Charles Rowland, pictured with his wife
Kate, when on leave in May 1918,
was killed three months later.

THE SPANISH 'FLU

For most healthy people an attack of influenza can be very unpleasant, but with the
introduction of annual vaccination for the elderly and not so fit, the virus is not the
killer it was. However, influenza should not be taken for granted, because there is
always the danger that one day an extremely lethal strain might emerge.

In 1957, the Asian 'flu epidemic killed up to a million people worldwide, and there
was another very nasty strain called Hong Kong 'flu in 1968; both of which I caught
and can confirm from first hand experience that they were very, very nasty!

The misnamed Spanish 'flu, which probably originated in China, turned into a
fearful pandemic in 1918, and although the total number of its victims is unknown, it
is believed that between 21 and 40 million of the world's people died; the virus killed
some 150,000 in England and Wales. Tragically, thousands of men of all nations, who
had survived the horrors of the First World War battlefields, were to fall victim to the
killer virus during the first months of peace.

The virus took hold of the patient quickly with a cough, headache and a raging
temperature of up to 104°F, and although many recovered, death could follow from
complications such as pneumonia for which there were no remedies.

In early July 1918, the first Yeovil cases were diagnosed in the Pen Mill area but
these were mild and all the patients recovered. Even so, the schools were closed on 16
July for several weeks but thankfully the outbreak was over by the middle of August.

The 'flu erupted again with a vengeance in the second week of October; and this time the virus was very nasty. It began once again in the Pen Mill area, probably brought in by railway workers going from town to town and mixing with infected passengers, and spread rapidly across Yeovil. On 21 and 22 October, all the day and Sunday Schools were closed and by the end of the month, factories and shops were short handed; the Borough Council's departments, most of which were engaged in trying to fight the infection, were so depleted of staff that they almost ceased functioning. The Albany Ward Picture Palace in the Triangle was closed to children and dances were cancelled.

The epidemic reached its height during November, then gradually faded away and had practically disappeared by Christmas. The virus in this second phase was the very dangerous strain, and the pneumonia which could rapidly develop, caused nearly all the deaths in the town. It was recorded that nose bleeding was a prominent symptom among children. Whole families could be simultaneously attacked and often there was great difficulty in getting them assistance. Help from relatives and friends was often not available as nearly every home in Yeovil was affected. Both of the town's District Nurses went down with the virus and tragically, twenty-six-year-old Nurse Gary died on 4 November, her condition being aggravated, by attending a 'flu patient when she was very ill herself. A few days earlier on 1 November, Mr J. H. MacMillan, a Voluntary Aid Detachment member working in the Red Cross Military Hospital in the Newnam Memorial Hall in South Street, also succumbed to the virus. The nurses working at Westlands were brought in to help the town medical authorities and the local doctors were put under tremendous pressure. One physician was away on military service, several went down with the flu and the town's Medical Officer of Health, Dr Weaver, found himself attending many of his private colleagues' patients who would otherwise have been without medical aid.

By the end of November the epidemic began to abate and schools and public places were re-opening, although the national Influenza Regulations which came into force on 18 November prohibited entertainments for longer than three hours without an interval of half an hour for the thorough ventilation of the room.

The total number of deaths in Yeovil in which influenza was certified as the primary or secondary cause was eighty-one divided almost equally between the sexes, forty males and forty-one females. The age group twenty-two to twenty-nine with twenty-two deaths was the highest and at each end of the generations there were fatalities; one an infant under a year and one 100-year-old Yeovilian. Mr H. St Clair, the manager of Albany Ward's Picture Palace, was one of the eighty-one deaths.

Captain Hucks RAF, who flew the first aircraft from Westland's airfield (as well as being the first Englishman to fly an aircraft upside down and loop the loop) died at Bourne End from pneumonia following influenza.

The onset of the deadly Spanish 'flu coincided with the end of the First World War and the outpouring of relief across the nation and Europe seems to have pushed this terrible epidemic into the back of folk memory. However, the eighty-one Yeovilians who died from the Spanish 'flu, sixty-three passing away in three weeks, outnumbers those who died in the bombing of the town during the Second World War.

A victim of the Spanish 'Flu - the headstone in Yeovil Cemetery of Herbert Alfred Griffin, or as he was better known, Herbert St Clair, manager of Mr Albany Ward's Picture Palace.

SEPTEMBER

By September 1918, the stalemate of the terrible trench warfare which had lasted nearly four years on the Western Front had been broken, and the Allied Armies had begun the advance which would lead to the end of hostilities two months later on 11 November.

At 5.33 in the morning of Tuesday 3 September 1918, following a three minute artillery and machine gun barrage, A and B companies of the 2nd Battalion, the Wiltshire Regiment, attacked German positions north-west of the village of Neuve-Chapelle some fifteen kilometres from Lille in northern France. The regimental history records that the attack progressed according to the programme, the Germans were taken completely by surprise, and the final objective of the crossroads known as 'Rouge Croix' was reached. Casualties were said to have been relatively small, six men killed and eighteen wounded. One of the men of A company attacking the position was my father who had served with the battalion since the previous April. The Commanding Officer of the 2nd Battalion was Lieutenant Colonel, Lord Thynne DSO, MP, who would be killed instantly eleven days later on 14 September.

Meanwhile back in Yeovil, in common with many other families across the nation, my grandparents were trying to carry on as normal, but with constant dread in the back of their minds of the news that their only son would not be coming home. They did receive a telegram several weeks later but this was to say that he had been wounded and was in hospital.

On 6 September, the *Western Gazette* in its column 'Yeovil and the War' wrote that

Lance-Corporal E. B. Way, of the Dorset Regt., whose wife lives at 118 Goldcroft, has been killed in action in France. He was 30 years of age, and had joined up on July 20th 1916, and was drafted to France in November of the same year. For 13 years he was engaged in the piano and music warehouse of Messrs Godfrey & Co., the Triangle, and was very well known. Mrs Way received notification from the Record Office that her husband was wounded, but later received a letter from a chaplain to a Canadian unit to the effect that Lance-Corporal Way had been killed in the recent advance, and that his body had been buried in a wheat field behind the present front line. The chaplain added that he had apparently been killed by a machine gun bullet whilst gallantly advancing on the battlefield, and that death had been evidently been instantaneous.

The *Gazette* also reported that

Private F. Peaty, RMLI, who will be remembered in Yeovil as a prominent footballer of a few seasons back, is again wounded, and is in hospital in Stoke-on-Trent, suffering from wounds to his left forearm. Private Peaty, whose wife lives in St Michael's Road, was wounded a few months ago, but was then treated in hospital in France and sent back to the front line.

Mr C. Dade of 10 South Western Terrace, Yeovil, has received news that his grandson, Private C. Samways, West Somerset Yeomanry, attached to the Somerset

Light Infantry, has been wounded in the head during the recent fighting in France. The news came in letters in which Private Samways states that his steel helmet was the means of saving his life. He says that his wound is slight and he is in hospital in Warrington in Lancashire. His letters are written in a very cheerful strain and Private Samways expresses a hope that he will be soon home again.

Mrs Bell of 22 Everton Road told the *Western Gazette* that she had received a postcard dated 23 June from her husband George, the former Boots at the Mermaid Hotel, who had been serving with Worcester Regiment and was now a prisoner of war in Germany. George stated that he was in the best of health but that being a prisoner of was not very nice. They were short of cigarettes and tobacco, and it was 'not like home.'

Meanwhile on the home front, the *Gazette* reported that the regular ambulance train had arrived at Sherborne on 6 September, and thirty-six wounded and gassed men straight from the front line were removed and taken to several local hospitals. Seven cases were brought to Yeovil, three being taken to the Red Cross Hospital and the remaining four to the District Hospital. On the day before, seventeen wounded soldiers recovering in the Red Cross Hospital were entertained at a picnic given by the staff of Wests, the outfitters and milliners shop in Middle Street. A Variety Concert in aid of the Red Cross was given to a large audience in the Assembly Rooms by 'the well-known troupe of pierrots under the management of Mr Libbis N. Burch of Chard.' The shows presented by this amateur concert party were very popular in the area and with its programme of songs, humour and dance, raised many hundreds of pounds for the Red Cross.

The Revd Edward Brentall, MA, opened his ministry of the Yeovil Wesleyan Circuit, with a service in the Vicarage Street Methodist Church, and was later welcomed at a united evening service of the town's free churches.

Yeovil Gloves featured in a large display at the Glasgow British Industries Fair, which was reported to 'have fully demonstrated the ability of English manufacturers to produce an article to suit every taste and requirement'.

The enforcement of Government regulations relating to the registration of aliens could cause problems. Early in September, a citizen of the United States of America, Mr O. Frick, an engineer, and his British-born artist wife, appeared before the magistrates charged with failing to register at the Yeovil police station as aliens under the Defence of the Realm Regulations, when they arrived in the town in the previous March. Mr Frick had been employed in the Aeronautical Department of Westland Aircraft and had worked for the War Office since the beginning of the war in 1914. Mr Frick's solicitor told the Bench that his client had informed Westlands of his nationality and having so notified all the authorities for whom he had previously worked, he did not realise that he had to register with the local police as well. Accepting that this had been an unintentional oversight the magistrates dismissed the case.

Shortage of labour had several times postponed the washing of the medium of the filter beds at the town sewage works, and at their September meeting the Borough Council decided to seek the employment of German prisoners of war for this task.

On 6 September 1918, the *Western Gazette* reported that Battery Sergeant Major W.

Westland Aircraft Progress Staff in 1918
Left to right; Mr Rymell, ?, Mr Evans, Mr Lower, Mr Sweet and Mr Portus (Head of Department).

Brice, Royal Garrison Artillery, of Yeovil, had been awarded the Distinguished Conduct Medal for 'conspicuous gallantry and devotion to duty during recent operations.'

THE WAR IS OVER!

At 11 o'clock on the morning of Monday the 11 November 1918, a great silence fell across the battlefields of France and Belgium as the guns stopped firing; the war was over. During the 1,561 days which had passed, from the day Great Britain declared war on Germany and her Allies, several thousand Yeovilians had served their country in all the theatres of war on land, sea and in the air. Over 220 had been killed or died from wounds or disease, and hundreds more had been wounded.

Thankfully the influenza outbreak appeared to be abating but not before it had killed the 'bright and cheery' Nurse Garry, who had 'answered a call for assistance from one of her patients when she herself was in need of the services of a nurse, and despite a plucky fight she succumbed'.

There was some excitement when at midday on Saturday the 2nd November 'a big service bi-plane made a forced landing in a mangold field near the Hollands Inn. The roots entangling the chassis caused the machine to somersault, and the occupant,

Lieutenant Alexander, had a narrow escape from injury'.

The Yeovil Men's section of the Somerset Voluntary Aid Detachment (VAD), were called out on two occasions to bring wounded soldiers from Sherborne Station to the Red Cross Hospital. The Men's VAD also entertained the wounded in the Hospital to an evening of whist, songs and music followed by light refreshments.

In the Borough there was a crowded open-air film show given from the back of a motor van sponsored by the Ministry of National Service. The programme included films of the Western Front and the work of the Royal Navy in hunting submarines in the seas around Great Britain. Ex-Corporal Stephen Scott of the Royal Warwickshire Regiment provided the commentary to the films about the Western Front and told the large audience of 'the atrocities of the Germans'. He also 'appealed to the workers to sink their grievances till the war was over, and not to strike to secure them by sacrificing the lives of the men fighting for them'. The *Western Gazette* reported that the purpose of the films was 'to bring home to the people the many aspects of the war'.

For many Yeovilians however, it did not need a free film to bring home, 'the many aspects of the war'. Mr and Mrs Jeffs of 7 Smiths Terrace were notified that their son Fred had been wounded in the chest by a shell splinter, and Mr William Salisbury of 34 Great Western Terrace heard that his son was in hospital in France. Prisoner of war, Private George Firebrance wrote home to his family at 76 Southville saying that he had received no parcels from Yeovil or England. Mrs Sugg of 15 Market Street received the dreaded telegram telling her that her husband William had died of 'a gas shell wound'; he was thirty-seven and left five young children. Borough Alderman Matthews was informed that his son Second Lieutenant Wilfred Matthews had been killed leading an attack on a German position. His death left a young widow, the fourth daughter of Mr and Mrs R. Bicknell of Allingham House, Yeovil. Lieutenant Matthews was posthumously awarded the Military Cross for his gallantry in leading the attack and tragically was the third son of Alderman and Mrs Matthews to be killed in the War.

Despite the constant worry about loved ones serving on the Western Front and in the other theatres of war, food shortages and an influenza epidemic, life still went on with some semblance of normality. The Editor of the *Western Gazette* presented Mr F. Clinker 'an old and valued employee' with a wallet containing 'treasury notes' to mark his Golden Wedding and 'wished him and Mrs Clinker more years of happy married life. Mr Clinker's feelings prevented him from replying.

Corporal William Waygood of Roping Path married Miss Ethel Wheeler of Hillgrove Avenue in St John's Church. The best man was Rifleman Dell 'both the bride's brothers being on active service and unable to be present.' The honeymoon was spent in Weston-super-Mare.

At the bankruptcy hearing of engineer Walter Austin of 24 Vincent Street, it was stated that he had liabilities of £412 but no assets, and he had never kept accounts.

The South Street Baptist Church celebrated its 230th anniversary and at a public meeting, the guest speaker the Reverend Charles Brown, past President of the National Free Church Council, 'looked forward to the time when people who tried to make war would be looked upon as criminals and men like the Supreme War Lords who brought war upon the world should be locked up in a madhouse'.

At their November meeting the Yeovil Education Committee were informed that in October, the boys of Reckleford School had picked 652 lbs of blackberries and the girls 441 lbs.

In its first November edition, the *Western Gazette* reported that a road traffic accident occurred in Preston Road at the junction with Grove Avenue when

a Rover car, belonging to Mr B. W. Male and driven by a lady, was going in the direction of Preston and reached the corner just as a closed Ford car, owned by Mr J. H. Swaffield, turned out of Grove Avenue. Both drivers did their best to avoid the other, but a collision occurred, the Rover car running in under the forepart of the Ford, and only a severe impact with wall outside Mr C. B. Benson's house saved this vehicle from overturning. The Ford car was conveying a man who had been taken ill at Westland to the hospital and he was rather badly shaken, and a man accompanying him was slightly cut about the face and neck with glass splinters from the smashed windows. A passing trap picked them up and conveyed them to the hospital. Considerable difficulty was experienced in getting the cars apart, one of the wheels of the Ford, which was the more damaged, having to be removed before they could be cleared. Beyond a twisted mudguard the other was little the worse and was able to proceed.

However, on 15 November, the *Gazette* could report that

On the posting of the telegrams at the newspaper offices announcing the signing of the armistice the news spread like wildfire on Monday morning, and those in the outlying parts of the town and others who had not heard of the telegrams got their first intimation from a visiting aeroplane decorated with streamers in the national colours, and which performed some extraordinary evolutions over the town. The flags on the Town Hall were quickly hoisted by Mr H. Jesty, and under his direction, and with the ready assistance afforded to him, the centre of the town was soon wreathed in bunting. Following this lead flags and streamers of every kind, some of them showing the effects of four years storage, made their appearance in all directions, and it is long since the town looked so festive. By mid-day work had been practically abandoned and the streets gradually filled, flags and national colours being carried by nearly everyone. The bells in the Parish Church tower added their note to the rejoicing, which was everywhere of a restrained character. The losses of Yeovil men have been too great and the appearance of the motor ambulances of the Men's VAD filled with wounded men being taken to the Red Cross Hospital, while provoking a sympathetic cheer, helped to remind the thankful crowds of the sterner side of the war.

On that Monday evening there was a packed town meeting to give thanks for the signing of the Armistice and the next day St John's Church was filled to capacity for the Service of Thanksgiving. The Great War was over, during which the lives of all Yeovilians had been affected but now, the town would have to manage the peace.

Postscript

HIGH STREET, YEOVIL.

A packed meeting in the Town Hall gave thanks for the signing of the Armistice.

The fighting and killing had stopped at the eleventh hour on 11 November 1918, but the *Western Gazette* sadly recorded on 22 November that

The deepest sympathy has been expressed with Mr and Mrs Hockey, of Pen Field, Sherborne Road, who, during the Armistice rejoicings, received the news of the death of their son, Private H. Hockey, of the Machine Gun Corps, who was killed only two days before the cessation of hostilities. The deceased was well known, and the news of his death at the age of twenty-four was received with regret. He had only been married about five months. The news was received by Mrs Hockey through a letter from the Major of her husband's Company, who writing expressing sympathy in the heavy blow she had sustained, says he was instantly killed with several of his comrades by the explosion of a mine near Avesnes, a town which he had gallantly helped to capture and was buried with several others in a field near the town. The late Private Hockey joined the Forces on 11th April last, and was drafted to France on 9th October, having thus served abroad only one month. The deceased was previously employed as a clerk by the Phoenix Engineering Co. Ltd., Chard, and was also a keen footballer.

CHRISTMAS 1918
AN ELECTION, A BRAWL AND GERMAN GUNS

For many pre-war years up to and including Christmas 1914, the *Western Gazette* had given detailed and fulsome reports on the Christmas season and the days leading up to the festival of goodwill. After the four years of terrible conflict, I had anticipated that Christmas 1918 would be fully reported and something of a return to the pre-war celebration. However, the report in the *Gazette* of 27 December 1918 could not have been further removed from those cheerful pre-war articles, and here it is.

> Christmas in Yeovil was again a quiet one. Numbers of men were home on leave from the Army and Navy, but otherwise few people were travelling. The postal pressure was as great as usual, and was dealt with by staff augmented by special helpers.

And there it was, but being realistic, I suppose that a nation which had suffered so much, and lost so many of its menfolk, was recovering from one of the worst and deadliest influenza epidemics in recorded history, and was in the midst of severe food and commodity rationing, could not be expected to return to celebratory mode. The great outpouring of relief and joy at the Armistice on the previous 11 November had probably emptied the national resource of emotion.

So what was going on during those few days of Christmas in December 1918?

One event which stands out, was the General Election held on 14 December, and which resulted a win for the Conservatives. Colonel Aubrey Herbert, Yeovil's Conservative MP since 1911 was returned polling 10,522 votes compared with 7,583 for Mr Kelly, the Labour candidate and 2,743 for the Liberal, Mr Brough. This was the first General Election at which women over thirty years of age were given the vote, but it would be another ten before the franchise was extended to all women over twenty-one.

Because of Christmas the counting of votes was deferred until Saturday, 28 December, and following the declaration of the Yeovil Division result from Town Hall at 1 p.m., a cheering crowd carried Colonel Herbert shoulder high into Princes Street, where a soldier insisted on carrying the Colonel on his back to the Assembly Rooms for the victory celebrations. From the Assembly Rooms, the Colonel accompanied by Mrs Herbert, were conducted back to the Mermaid Hotel, for lunch with prominent supporters and local dignitaries. Later that afternoon the couple took their seats in a large limousine which was then pulled through the main streets by teams of soldiers and sailors, before the Colonel and his lady were driven to Coker Court as guests of Colonel and Mrs Godfrey Heneage.

On Monday 23 December, an Australian soldier, Private Chilvers, appeared before the town magistrates, charged with assaulting PC Willment on the previous Saturday and refusing to leave licensed premises when ordered to do so.

Constable Willment told the Bench that he had been called to the Railway Tavern in Middle Street on Saturday evening and found the prisoner drunk and causing a disturbance. When told to stop, the soldier had let loose a string of 'filthy language' and when asked to produce his leave pass, refused and threatened to shoot the constable with 'a six-shooter he had in hip pocket'. As the soldier went for his hip pocket PC Willment stated that he had grabbed his arm but was hit several times on the chest, but eventually managed to get handcuffs on the prisoner's wrists and took him into custody. No gun was being carried.

Mr George Hoare, the licensee told the Bench that when the Australian had come into the inn, he had been very drunk and he had refused to serve him. The soldier had then become disorderly but as he had refused to leave the police were called.

In his defence, Private Chilvers stated that he had been in the army four years and had never been asked by a civilian to show his pass. He had been upset and considered the constable's actions in trying to handcuff him to be unwarranted. However, he pleaded guilty to both charges,

The chairman of the Bench told the accused that he had committed a very serious offence and could go to prison for three months. The Bench was, however, prompted to take a lenient view as it was Christmas and fined Private Chilvers fifteen shillings for the assault and five shillings for failing the leave the inn.

On 1 January 1919, two 77 mm German field guns, captured on the Western Front and now on tour in Somerset, were hauled by motor lorries into the Borough where they remained on public show for two days. The guns proved a magnet for the town youngsters resulting in the *Western Gazette* commenting that 'many people found difficulty in seeing an outline of the guns owing to youngsters which crowded every bit of space possible to clamber on'.

Following his election success, Colonel Aubrey Herbert, MP, and Mrs. Herbert were entertained to lunch in the Mermaid Hotel.

The First Years of Peace

PEACE DAY 1919

The Armistice which ended the fighting on the Western Front on 11 November 1918 was not the official end of the First World War, and it was not until the Peace Treaty was signed at Versailles in France on 28 June 1919, that the War was finally declared to be over.

Saturday, 19 July 1919 was the day when peace celebrations would be held throughout Great Britain and the Empire – Peace Day.

The month had started hot and dry, so in Yeovil outdoor sports, games and parties were the order of the day. However, the British climate lived up to its reputation, and the morning of Peace Day dawned with torrential rain which continued for most of the day.

Punctually at 6 a.m., the bells of St John's Church rang out across the town and detonations from a canon heralded the start of the celebrations. At 10 a.m., a procession was formed near Sidney Gardens, and marched off to the United Drumhead Service in Wyndham Fields led by the Salvation Army Band and followed by the Mayor and Corporation, about 700 ex-servicemen, war widows, the Yeovil Town Band, Men's VAD, khaki-clad members of the 1st Wessex Boys' Brigade Bugle Band, Boy Scouts, Girl Guides, the police, the Westland Works Band and several hundred townspeople. The *Western Gazette* commented that the ex-servicemen marched with 'the characteristic British Army swing but it was a sad fact that few were there who had marched away amid the cheers and the band playing of the early days of 1914.' Unfortunately the Yeovil Fire Brigade could not take its place in the parade as it had been called to a fire at Chilthorne Domer.

Several thousand people had already gathered in Wyndham Fields, and following the Service of Thanksgiving the ex-servicemen and war widows reformed, and at half-past eleven marched back in the rain through the town, along Huish and Orchard Street to the Westland Aircraft Works and the Civic Welcome and Luncheon in one of the large hangars. Following a warm welcome from the Mayor, Councillor

Despite the rain, several thousand townspeople gathered on Wyndham Fields for the Service of Thanksgiving.

W. R. E. Mitchelmore, the ex-servicemen and war widows sat down to the luncheon which began with the mayor carving a round of beef with the sword used for carving the joint at the Great Peace Rejoicings held in Yeovil in 1815 following the Battle of Waterloo.

The heavy rain meant that the sports programme and most of the outdoor events had to be postponed for a week, and the arrangements for the children's part of the festival were drastically altered. The plan had been for around 2,000 youngsters to assemble in and around St John's Churchyard, and enjoy a musical programme. Then they would march to Westland Works for tea. Instead the children assembled in their schools, and the tea, which had been prepared in the Westland canteen, was packed up and distributed by motor lorry.

However, the weather did not affect the Saturday evening entertainment by Mr Carlton Frederick's Sunbeam Costume Concert Party in one of the large Westland hangars. Although the rain did not prevent the bonfire being lit on Summerhouse Hill at 10.45 p.m., some local yobs almost put paid to the event by stealing most of the wood during the preceding week. The town's Boy Scouts, however, came out in force to gather replacement material, but sadly the fire was not on the scale intended.

THE SPOILS OF WAR

There are many older Yeovilians who may still remember the German gun which stood in Bide's Garden (now forming part of the Reckleford dual carriageway) during the years before the Second World War, and which was taken away to be melted down as scrap iron for the war effort. At the meeting of the Yeovil Borough Council in December 1918, the mayor reported that a letter had been received from the Secretary of the War Office Trophies Committee stating that the allocation of captured German guns to towns throughout the country was now under consideration. Regiments who had substantiated their claims to captured guns were being asked by the Trophies Committee for their wishes about the allocation of these war trophies. The mayor then read a letter from the Major commanding the Somerset Light Infantry Depot at Taunton stating that it was impossible at the moment to say how the German guns captured by the Regiment would be allocated within the county. However, a town the size of and importance of Yeovil would stand high on the Regiment's list when the time came to decide the allocation. And so the matter rested.

In the meantime, however, at the Council's meeting in April 1919, the members were informed that the National War Savings Committee had offered the town the gift of a heavy tank in recognition of the £600,000 raised in War Bonds by the Yeovil War Savings

The German gun stood in Bide's Garden until it was removed when the Second World War broke out in September 1939.

Committee. Councillor Petter, the chairman of the town's Savings Committee proposed that the offer be accepted and suggested that the tank would be a lasting memorial to one of the many efforts made during the war. The Council was advised that the tank was 30 feet long, 13 feet wide and weighed about 26 tons. The tank would have to be placed on a very substantial base to be constructed at the Council's expense and it was suggested that the Sidney Gardens might be a suitable site. After some discussion the offer was referred to the Improvement Committee for consideration, but three months later they reported that no suitable site could be found and the offer was declined with thanks.

At the Council's meeting in November 1919. the mayor reported a letter had been received from the Marquis of Bath, the Lord Lieutenant of Somerset, stating that a captured German howitzer gun had been allocated to Yeovil, and would be dispatched shortly from Taunton.

Councillor Higdon, remarked that some time ago he understood the Council had been promised one of the guns captured by the 6th Battalion, the Somerset Light Infantry. He believed that there were only twelve men remaining from this battalion, and Mr Fenwick, the manager of the Town Gas Works, was one of them. Councillor Higdon reminded members that the Sixth Battalion had fought nobly for the trophy, and it would be very valuable if the town could obtain this gun because they were entitled to it. However, the mayor pointed out that the gun referred to had been recaptured by the Germans in their advance in March 1918 when the enemy went back over the ground where the guns were standing!

Councillor Petter proposed that the gun, when it was received, should be temporarily placed in the Triangle until a more appropriate site could be found, and in 1922 it was removed to Bide's Garden where it remained until the Second World War.

THE WAR MEMORIALS

Yeovil Borough

Shortly after the War broke out in August 1914, the Yeovil Borough Council decided that there should be a memorial to honour those Yeovilians who gave their lives in the service of their country, but no one could have foreseen the terrible four years which would follow. However, on 9 November 1918, two days before the Armistice brought the war to an end, the Council resolved to take, 'The necessary steps to compile a list of all Yeovil officers and men who have fallen in the war, for the purpose of inscribing their names in a roll of honour for the town after the conclusion of hostilities.'

A War Memorial Committee was set up, the design finally agreed, and the Council decided that the most appropriate site for the memorial was in the Borough. At 6 o'clock in the evening of Thursday 15 July 1921, the war memorial, with 226 names, was unveiled and dedicated before a large crowd of Yeovilians gathered in the Borough. The 29 feet high spire-shaped cross was designed by a Yeovil man, Mr Wilfred Childs, and made by Messrs Appleby & Childs a firm of Yeovil monumental masons, from the finest Ham Hill stone. The memorial was draped with the Union Flag and a White Ensign made by Miss M. Cooper and Miss Edith Childs. Describing the ceremony the

When the memorial was dedicated in the Borough on 15 July 1921, veterans wearing their medals proudly stood in respectful memory of their fallen comrades.

Western Gazette wrote that:

Yeovil Territorial Company under the command of Captain J. R. Ware, marched in first and took up a position, and they were soon followed by a large contingent of ex-servicemen, headed by the Town Band, who marched in from Middle Street. These veterans, many of who were wearing their medals, kept the ground - a hollow square before the flag covered cross, and with the police, did much towards preserving the quietude and order before the service. Then came a pathetic little procession into the square, a large party of children, many of them tiny tots, carrying posies of flowers, which they were to place later on the base of the Monument on which was engraved the names of their fathers. Just after the town clock struck the hour the final procession moved through the crowd. Headed by the clergy and ministers of all denominations it included the Mayor, and Aldermen and Councillors of Yeovil Corporation.

'The hymn 'Nearer My God to Thee' was sung and the Mayor, Alderman W. R. E. Mitchelmore, addressed the crowd. He said that the memorial was a token of love, respect and gratitude for the sacrifice made by those whose names were inscribed upon it and would be a shrine here in Yeovil for the men whose graves were scattered far and wide. At the call of the mayor, Lieutenant Colonel F. D. Urwick, DSO, who had seen distinguished service with the Somerset Light Infantry in the Middle East, pulled a cord and the flags fell away. The Vicar of Yeovil then dedicated the memorial, a hymn and the National Anthem concluded the ceremony.

Yeovil Borough

5 WAR MEMORIAL, YEOVIL

During the years which followed the names became eroded and bronze panels bearing the names were fixed to the memorial faces and another ten names of the First World War fallen were added. The Yeovil Town Council have since added to the memorial, the names of those who fell in the Second World War, both service and civilian, and a serviceman who died during the Falklands conflict in 1982.

Preston Plucknett

Until the boundaries of the Borough of Yeovil were extended westward in 1929, Preston Plucknett was a separate parish, and at a parish meeting held in the school in October 1919, it was agreed that a war memorial cross should be placed on a prominent position in the village. A house-to-house collection raised the sum of £170 for the memorial which took the form of a Ham Hill stone cross, based on a similar cross in the churchyard of Holy Trinity Church, Shaftesbury. The memorial was placed in the orchard owned by Mr R. Ponsonby of Brympton D'Evercy and occupied by Mrs Hawkins, opposite the old Post Office and adjoining the road to Yeovil.

On Tuesday evening 6 July 1920, the memorial was dedicated in the presence of a large number of villagers and people from Yeovil. The cross standing on a rectangular block upon which was carved the names of the fifteen men of the village who had lost their lives in the war, was made by the Ham Hill Company from its finest stone. A procession of twenty former soldiers, commanded by ex-Sergeant E. A. Stagg, left St James' Church followed by the church choir, the Vicar of Yeovil-with-Preston, the Revd H. C. Sydenham, and Churchwardens, and marched to the memorial where they formed a guard of honour around the cross which was draped with the Union Flag and the White Ensign. Following the singing of the hymn 'Nearer My God to Thee' the flags were removed by two ex-servicemen, more hymns were sung, prayers led by the Vicar and several addresses were given. The service concluded with the National Anthem and the Last Post sounded by ex-Bugle-Major Donovan of Yeovil and ex-Private Beaton of East Coker. Flowers and wreaths were placed on the steps of the memorial and villagers and friends filed past.

The names of two local men who died in the Second World War have been inscribed on the war memorial which was set back to its present position following road widening some years ago.

STORIES FROM THE WAR MEMORIAL

Here are the stories behind a few of the names of those who did not come home from the Great War.

From the *Western Gazette* 1 September 1916:

> Lionel Vaughan aged 27, the eldest son of Mr W. F. Vaughan, Great Western Railway's stationmaster at Yeovil was killed in France on the Somme Front. He has many friends in Bridport and Yeovil, where he is well-known. He served with General

Preston Plucknett

Botha through the campaign and eventual conquering of German South West Africa in the Veterinary Corps. When this German Colony was vanquished he proceeded to German East Africa under General Smuts, where he was selected with sixteen others, to go to France as a sniper, he being a particularly fine shot. With others they formed the S.A. Sharpshooters Section, and were attached to the Northamptonshire Regiment, 2nd Brigade. After spending a few days home in Yeovil recently, he was ordered to the Front, where he has remained under the command of Lieut. Methliven, who has written a deeply sympathetic letter to the bereaved parents expressing the regret of his comrades and bearing tribute to his gentlemanly conduct and bravery in the field. It should be mentioned that the deceased gave up a good appointment in Rhodesia to fight for King and country. His younger brother is now serving in the West Somerset Yeomanry.

From the *Western Gazette* 27 October 1916:

Sympathy is felt for Mr and Mrs Chudleigh, of Braeside, Grove Avenue, Yeovil, in the loss of their son Private J.E. Chudleigh, who has been killed in action in France. 'Jack' as he was familiarly known amongst a host of friends in Yeovil, was only 19 years of age. He joined the London Scottish about eight months ago, previous to which he belonged to the Yeovil Volunteers, joining at the start, and holding the rank of section commander, and his genial disposition and *bonhomie* made him exceedingly popular in the platoon, amongst the members of which his memory will be long cherished, From an early age until his voice broke, Jack Chudleigh was a chorister at the parish church, and was one of the most popular members of the choir. He was also a member of the Yeovil Male Voice Choir. He was a lad of fine physique, and the splendid tribute paid to the deceased by his Commanding Officer and the knowledge that their son had won a coveted distinction on the field of battle, not long before he paid the supreme sacrifice, will no doubt afford some consolation to the parents in their hour of grief.

The letter received from the deceased's Commanding Officer gives the reason for the long delay in giving his parents the sad information. The writer adds:- 'On the evening of September 19th this Company had an exceedingly difficult task to perform, which necessitated the whole Company moving across an area sniped by the enemy. Captain H. L. Lyer, who was leading and in command of the Company, was the first to be hit, and was dangerously wounded. It fell to me then to "carry on." Your son was acting as "runner" to me, and was wounded soon after we started. As I was by him I know that the wound was not serious, for he left me to find his way to the aid post, and I naturally reported him wounded. After that date we took part in many other such enterprises and attacks, and it was only at the beginning of this month that your son's platoon sergeant handed me the pay-book and pocket-book belonging to your son. This was given to him by a man, a -----company stretcher bearer, who was then down at the base for a rest. This man had had them handed to him by a perfect stranger to him telling him they had been taken from your son's body. No other information was given but that man stated your son was certainly dead. This company stretcher bearer returned only yesterday, and it was then that he gave me the latter information, because I had before hoped that your son's jacket had been taken off to dress the wound, and these articles were later found by someone. I have made enquiries for the man who originally found your son's body, but can get no trace of him, and can only conclude that man has also since become a casualty.

I cannot speak too highly of your late son. On many occasions he carried messages through difficult and dangerous parts, and went out on patrols and reconnaissance work often because he was found to be so reliable, and showed great courage on all occasions. It is feared that on his way to the medical aid post, he must have been hit again, this causing his death. He was a great favourite in the Company, and Capt. Lyer thought no end of him, in fact he recommended him for an award, and I am proud to tell you that the Military Medal was awarded to him a short while ago, though too late, unfortunately for your gallant son to wear. Assuring you of the fullest sympathy of all your son's comrades and officers, and trusting that the knowledge of his conspicuous bearing and good-hearted cheerfulness may be of comfort to you. – E.D. COLE, Lieut. Officer commanding --- Company --- London Scottish.'

At the parade of the Yeovil Volunteers last evening sympathetic allusion was made to the death of Private Chudleigh, and, as a mark of respect to the memory of the deceased, the 'Last Post' was sounded by Bugler Newton, the platoon standing at the 'present.'

Mr Chudleigh has another son in the Army, Trooper Leslie Chudleigh of the West Somerset Yeomanry, who joined up in 1914, was wounded in the Dardanelles and in hospital for three months, and who is now on service in Egypt. [He survived the War]

The Battle of Jutland fought on the North Sea on 31 May/1 June 1916, was the only time the British Grand Fleet and the German High Seas Fleet met in battle during the War. Two hundred and forty eight warships with over 70,000 seamen fought a battle which was considered to have been a tactical victory for the Germans, but a strategic victory for the British because following retirement to its home bases the German High Seas Fleet never ventured out again to engage the Grand Fleet. The British lost fourteen ships including the battle cruisers *Invincible*, *Queen Mary* and *Indefatigable* and armoured cruisers *Black Prince*, *Warrior* and *Defence* and other ships were damaged. The German High Seas Fleet lost eleven. The following three Yeovil men lost their lives during the battle:

Ordinary Seaman Ernest Cox from Camborne Street, HMS *Black Prince*;
Royal Marine Corporal Stanley Burrows, West Hendford, HMS *Indefatigable*:
Royal Marine Harwood Rendell, 78 Huish, HMS *Invincible*.

Seventeen-year-old *Private Walter Adams* of the Royal Marine Light Infantry was lost in the sinking of HMS *Hampshire*, off the Orkneys on 5 June 1916, and in the *Western Gazette* of the 9 June it was reported that

He was the son of Mrs L. Moseley (by her first husband) and grandson of Mr W. Bond, of 32 Crofton Avenue. Before joining the forces, he was employed at the

'Western Gazette' Offices, and was connected with the Sports Club, being a good runner, footballer and swimmer. On Wednesday morning a postcard was received from him saying that he had come through the great battle [Jutland] quite safe, and would write a long letter later.

In the following September the *Gazette* would report that Walter's body had been recovered and buried in the Naval Cemetery at Lyness in the Orkneys.

Cadet Douglas Marnie was a young Scotsman who had come to Yeovil to work as a pupil at the Goldcroft Glove Company but after joining the Royal Air Force in June 1918 was in training at a recruits' depot when he contracted the dreaded Spanish Influenza and passed away from pneumonia on 4 July aged just eighteen-and-a-half. Cadet Marnie was buried in the cemetery of Cathcart his home town.

On 19 July 1918 the *Western Gazette* reported that:

A memorial service to the late Cadet Douglas Marnie, RAF was held in the Princes Street Congregational Church on Sunday morning. The deceased was a keen worker with the BB Cadets as a lieutenant of the Company, and was also the Sunday School assistant secretary and a Worker in the Young People's Society. There was a large and sympathetic congregation, including the 1st, 2nd and 3rd Yeovil Boys' Brigade Companies, the Baptist Girls' Life Brigade and the Girl Guides. Appropriate music was played and suitable hymns sung, and during the service the Rev. R. Newell feelingly alluded to the following who had been associated with the Boys' Brigade, and who had given their lives for their country:- Bert Norman, Harry White (lieutenant of the Company), Clarence Tucker, Harry Holland, Stanley Purchase, Ernest Gatehouse and Frank Ostler. Brought up in the home of the Boys' Brigade movement - he had been member of one of the largest companies in Glasgow - and valued it very much, not only because of the drill, but because it was of a religious foundation and character, and aimed to make strong Christian men of the boys who were associated with it. He (the rev. gentleman) was sorry that the Boys' Brigade had changed its name to become the Cadet Corps, but he hoped that the Cadet Corps would never change its character, but that it would always remain a religious movement, and so long as the churches appointed its officers it would be so.

Air Mechanic 2nd Class, Maurice Poole, Royal Air Force, whose parents lived at 21 Orchard Street, died from double pneumonia at Abokir, Egypt on 25 June 1919. Aged eighteen he had been in the RAF only twelve months, eleven of which he had spent in Egypt. In a letter sent on 17 June, Maurice wrote that he was well and hoped to return home shortly. This was the second blow felt by Mr and Mrs Poole who had lost their elder son William from enteric fever at Basra Hospital on 14 September 1918 aged twenty; he was serving with the Northumberland Fusiliers.

EPILOGUE

I discovered this poem many, many years ago in a publication, the title of which I'm sorry to say I have no record, or recollection. Sufficient to say that I copied it, and it has remained a poem which I find especially moving. I have not been able to gather any information about Private Ivor Morgan, and I have not been able find any record in the Commonwealth War Graves Commission's database of him losing his life in the Great War. I hope he survived.

The 16th (Service) Battalion, Welsh Regiment (Cardiff City) to give the Battalion its correct title, was raised in Cardiff in November 1914 and was sent to the Western Front in December 1915. The Battalion saw much action, over 150 men were killed and some 300 wounded at the Battle of Mametz Wood on the Somme on 7 July 1916, and further heavy losses were experienced on the Western Front especially in the Third Battle of Ypres, or Passchendaele as this long drawn out battle in the late summer and autumn of 1917, has become known.

What's in the air? There's a murmuring note
Winding its way through the bugle's throat.
A sound in the distance far away,
Not very much in the air today.

What's in the air that travels so fast
Following the sound of that bugle's blast?
A sinister note of war's alarms
Louder and Clearer "To arms To arms!"

What's in the air? The soul-scaring tramp
Of armed soldiers marching to camp.
A rattle of bayonets, stern commands,
Martial music from military bands.

What's in the air? Oh strategic plans
And banquets for men from corned beef cans.
Oh yes, there's fever and dread disease
Mosquitoes, bluebottles, lice and fleas.

What's in the air? Loud thuds and wild yells,
Fire and flame and poison gas shells
Making a Hell of a world so gay
Oh yes, there's more in the air today.

Private Ivor Morgan, 16th Battalion (Cardiff Pals) The Welsh Regiment

The Band of the 4th Battalion of the Wiltshire Regiment in Yeovil in 1915.